THE PICTURE BOOK OF THE
USA
IN COLOR

Mary Moore Mason

DIADEM BOOKS

Published in the U.S.A. by Diadem Books
a division of the Barre Publishing Company, New York
by arrangement with

the Hamlyn Publishing Group Limited
London · New York · Sydney · Toronto
Astronaut House, Feltham, Middlesex, England

ISBN 0-517-125552
Library of Congress Catalog Card No. 74-83961

Printed in the United States of America

CONTENTS

Half title page *Central Park, New York*
Title page *Jackson Lake and Mt Moran, viewed from Leeks' Lodge, Wyoming*
Contents page *Haymaking in the Midwest*

AMERICA, OUR America—it is so easy to paint your portrait in bright, uncomplicated colors: in the red, white and blue of your flag, your hamburger stands, your parades or your old *Saturday Evening Post* covers; or in the stark black and white of your slums, racial problems and economic inequities. And yet, particularly today as you enter your third century of independence, you are a country both of vivid contrasts and pastel subtleties, of brilliant sun and sudden shadows, of vast cloudless landscapes and cluttered city scenes, of pretty floral print suburbs and harsh industrial collages, of faces demanding the aristocratic authority of a Sargent or Holbein, the satirical touch of a Hogarth or Daumier, the folksiness of a Norman Rockwell or the tragic knowledge of a Goya or Munch. Here, the fine lines of an etching are required; there, the indistinct flow of a water color. This mood calls for a spontaneous pencil sketch; that, for the impact of chisel against stone. Then, even as the paint dries or as the figure is born from the rock, the mood changes yet again; your portrait is once more incomplete.

The difficulties are not really surprising. The landscape painter must stretch his canvas across 3,615,123 square miles from the frozen tip of Point Barrow, Alaska, to Ka Lae in the southern tip of lush Hawaii, almost from the shores of Russia at Cape Wrangell in the Aleutian Islands to the rocky easternmost point of West Quoddy Head, Maine. He must be skilled at capturing the fiery summit of an Hawaiian volcano or the icy tip of Alaska's Mount McKinley; the violent glare of Death Valley or the gloom of a Great Smokies' forest; the ever-changing patterns of sunlight in the Grand Canyon or the artificial illumination of the Endless Caverns; the wide-open rippling plains of the Midwest or the Spanish-moss-swathed mysteries of the Deep Southern swamps; the sparkling clarity of a Rockies' mountain stream or the rancid pollution of a fish-bloated Great Lake.

The urban painter also has too wide a choice. Does he concentrate on the neat New England villages favored by greeting card manufacturers, the decaying southern towns and cities so dear to the hearts of novelists and playwrights or the dusty western crossroads forgotten by all except the film makers and a handful of historians? In brief: where can he really find Our Town, Main Street, U.S.A.? Must he be a cubist or an abstract expressionist to express the vertical thrust but downward pull of our great cities, the spiralling mazes of our motorways, the yawning conformity of some of our

Wherever you find Americans you find the flag: sedately hanging from a Manhattan mansion, fluttering with wild abandon over a modest farm house in a remote Colorado valley; streaming from the tail of a motorcycle racing down a Nevada highway or drooping limply in the hot southern sun over an Alabama school house; cheering on a joyful football crowd or consoling a soldier's widow standing in prayer by a flag-draped coffin; guiding Americans into the future of outer space or reminding them of their past, as in this picture from a New Mexico ceremonial march. Perhaps its particular poignance comes from those fifty glittering white stars resting on its blue field, for in spite of their differences and even a tragic Civil War, the fifty states which they represent have remained democratically united to form the fourth largest country in the world, a feat unrivalled in the history of mankind.

suburbs, the great beauty of others, the garish commercial lifeblood of our neon-lit arteries?

Or perhaps he would be best to express himself through social realism, presenting a panorama of paradoxes: warm hospitality and incredible violence; an obsession with our own history and a passion for replacing the old with the new; a genius for inventing some of the world's most useful—and destructive—objects and values; a passionate regard for our great scenic heritage and, until recently, a lack of concern at its desecration; a great belief in freedom as long as it does not permit someone who 'doesn't belong' to stroll through our fields, enjoy our beach or move into our suburb; an ability to produce some of the world's most sensational architecture and some of its more depressing slums; idealism enough to lead the world, corruption enough to stun it; the most vibrant and amazing democracy ever known to man, but still a country where the rich finance, and attempt to influence, political figures.

Such a panorama is, of course, impossible without people. Our artist might persuade an elegant socialite or a rich industrialist to sit for portraits surrounded by handsome manifestations of their wealth. He might catch some of Norman Rockwell's jolly small-town folk swapping stories in a back room somewhere or a disillusioned slum dweller sitting dispiritedly on his front stoop one hot August night, but for the most part your people are a restless people, seldom still enough for more than a quick sketch, moving continually back and forth across your vast country, more likely to be found in a sports car or on a tractor than posing heroically on a horse, more frequently to be seen rushing through a supermarket than playing a leisurely game of country store chess, more concerned with analyzing their own political problems than with being sketched from life.

Even if he were uninspired by your present scene, an artist could easily find his muse in your dramatic history, sometimes thrilling, sometimes tragic. But should he concentrate on your world-inspiring moments—Patrick Henry's call for 'liberty or death', the signing of the Declaration of Independence, Abraham Lincoln's Emancipation Proclamation, Woodrow Wilson's call for a League of Nations, Franklin Delano Roosevelt's promise of a 'New Deal', John Kennedy's battle cry for a 'New Frontier', the astronauts' first walk on the moon—or should he somberly paint the tragedies, the Civil War destruction of the South, the deprivation of Blacks and Indians, the Depression, the assassination of the Kennedy brothers and Martin Luther King, Watergate? But on what great canvas could he portray your greatest achievement: the ability of fifty quite different states containing nearly 209 million people democratically to establish and then retain the United States of America?

Yes, how do we paint your portrait? Our pallet is new, our colors are fresh and our brush is ready and then you turn, show us another side, appear in yet another light, making us realize that once again we have only captured your profile, a mere outline of the personality within.

8

Perhaps inspired by our
pioneer forefathers,
Americans are a nation of
tireless and interested
travelers. Be it by
America's modern Pony
Express – an air-conditioned
Greyhound Bus (*above*) –
train, car or motorcycle, we
are frequently on the move,
changing jobs, homes, even
families – or just admiring
one of the largest, most
beautiful and most diversified countries on earth: a
country that boasts some of
the world's largest and most
fertile flatlands and
mountains such as soaring
(10,778 feet), snow-capped
Mount Baker in northern
Washington (*left*); a
country that includes the
frenetic rush of some of the
world's largest cities and
the timeless charm of North
Carolina's garden-
garlanded Orton Plantation
(*below*); a country that has
in its relatively short
history developed to the
limits of its own geo-
graphical boundaries and
quite literally reached for
the moon.

The immense variety of scenery in the United States of America includes one of the most formidable spots on earth: Death Valley. At 282 feet below sea level, it is the lowest point in the western hemisphere; its maximum recorded temperature is 190°F, only 22 degrees below boiling point. Stretching for nearly 3,000 square miles of sun-baked, cracked earth and sand surrounded by stark sentinel buttes and mountains, even its place names reflect the grim sense of humor developed by its first visitors: The Devil's Golf Course (*above*), Dante's View, the Funeral Mountains. It is easy to imagine why some of the '49ers who wandered in here en route to the gold fields emerged half mad – if at all. Yet the place has an eerie beauty of shifting sand dunes up to 200 feet high, of unexpected animal tracks, of mountain ranges shimmering in the distance, among them snow-covered Mount Whitney, at 14,495 feet the highest point in the conterminous United States.

Not only is America a land of vast, sparsely populated wildernesses, it is a land of huge cities, containing three of the world's ten largest metropolitan areas. Of these, perhaps Chicago, second largest city, is the true capital. Located at the northern gateway to the country's huge, fertile heartland, it is one of the leading agricultural and industrial centers of the nation, and the hub of its transportation system, providing water access to the Atlantic and international markets through Lake Michigan, upon whose shores it is built, as well as access to the country's major riverways and railways and one of the world's busiest airports. Among those who have exulted in its very bigness and brassiness have been poet Carl Sandburg who called it his 'Stormy, husky, brawling, City of the Big Shoulders' and the architects who have created views such as this one (below) seen from the 1,127-feet John Hancock Center. Now that the Sears Tower, an awe-inspiring 1,450 feet, is completed, the city boasts three of the world's six tallest buildings as well as architectural masterpieces by Frank Lloyd Wright, Louis Sullivan and Mies van der Rohe.

THE GREAT WATERS
Lifeblood of a New World

FIRST THERE WAS THE great water—the dark unknown Atlantic—luring only the most adventuresome to a mysterious destiny through uncharted seas. They may have hoped to find the Grand Khan, the spices and glittering treasures of the Orient; what they did find was the 2,069-miles long, ever-changing Atlantic coast of what was to become the United States of America—its promontories like beckoning fingers, its great bays and rivers tempting them into the dangerous interior, its varied landscape, from the harsh rocky coasts of Maine to the warm, sandy beaches of Florida, molding their personality and their history.

Florida hung like a ripe fruit within reach of the Spaniards ravaging the Caribbean islands and South America, its promise unique: the secret of Eternal Youth. The scent of gold led Sir Francis Drake and the *Golden Hind* up the Pacific Coast past what was to become San Francisco, the Golden Gate of the Gold Rush nearly three centuries later. The great sponge of the Chesapeake Bay absorbed the passengers of the *Susan Constant, Godspeed* and *Discovery* into its malarial swamps where only the strongest survived to found the first permanent English colony of Jamestown, Virginia. The curved arm of Cape Cod gathered up the wandering Pilgrims and guided them to the first New England colony. The great funnel of the St Lawrence promised a northwest passage to the Orient and delivered the Great Lakes and eventually the Mississippi into the hands of French fur traders and explorers.

Wherever they steered their course—along the coastlines, up the wide rivers, across the immense lakes—these men contributed their tenacity, their courage and often their names and even their lives to the mapping of what was to become the world's fourth largest country.

But even as they claimed their sacrificial victims, the great waters, long worshipped by the Indians, rewarded those who tamed them. The deep river landings of the Deep South encouraged a feudal plantation life serviced by the floating palaces or river boats immortalized by Mark Twain, himself a former river pilot. The rocky coast of New England bred sailors and whalers hardy enough to profit against the fierce North Atlantic. The sinuous muddy Mississippi and its tributaries created a fertile agricultural basin of 1,250,000 square miles. The great Salt Lake of Utah appeared like

Wind-swept Lake Michigan, third largest lake in North America and sixth largest in the world, is the only one of the Great Lakes completely within the United States of America. First discovered by Jean Nicolet in 1634, the 22,400-square-miles body of water soon became a 307-mile-long major highway toward the sea for pioneers and later for agriculturalists and industrialists. It remains so today despite the abrupt, fierce storms which have been known to snap a 640-foot steel freighter in two. In all, the Great Lakes are the largest body of fresh water in the world, encompassing five of the world's fifteen largest lakes, washing the shores of one Canadian province and eight states, draining an area of 300,000 square miles, covering 96,000 square miles in surface and flowing to the sea at a rate of 240,000 cubic feet per second.

a mirage to guide the persecuted Mormons to a site for their City of the Saints.

The five Great Lakes, numbered among the world's fifteen largest, with their outlets to Canada and the Atlantic, encouraged the construction of great industrial cities such as Detroit, Chicago and Cleveland. The very majesty of their settings, plus certain practicalities, inspired engineers to mold metal into the poetry of San Francisco's Golden Gate Bridge, to moor the Florida Keys to the mainland with a long concrete chain, to site a huge Statue of Liberty bearing a welcoming torch in the midst of New York Bay. The powerful rivers and waterfalls produced both tourist attractions such as the Grand Canyon and Niagara Falls and electricity for cities and industry. The sunny shores of southern Florida inspired turn-of-the-century entrepreneurs to sculpt canals and marinas, skyscraper hotel sites and swimming pools from what had been deserted sand bars. Huge dams like the Hoover brought lakes to the desert. The shipyards and harbors produced and protected the world's largest navy, and the rivers, lakes and oceans produced—and when not polluted, continue to produce—the basic ingredients for such succulent delicacies as shrimp creole, Oysters Rockefeller, San Francisco's cioppino stew, trout amandine, New England clam chowder and Huck Finn's famous fried catfish. Perhaps the most noticeable to the average American, the grandiose and the gentle waters of our country produce a liquid poem to the beauty of America, an ever-changing playground for those weary of the concrete realities of city life.

And what poetry, what variety! From Michigan's 'rushing Taquamenaw', home of Longfellow's Hiawatha, to the quiet New England pond which inspired Thoreau. From Mark Twain's wide, muddy Mississippi, 2,348 miles long, to the sinuous shimmering Snake fed by the melting ice of the Grant Teton. From the perilous New England, Oregon and Washington coasts swept by fogs, kamikaze squads of mewing seagulls and sentinel lighthouses' beams to the soft, hot sand of the southern Atlantic and Pacific coasts. From quiet New York State trout streams flowing under old covered bridges to the raging surf of Hawaii or of California. From the country's deepest lake, in an extinct Oregon crater, to the shallow swamplands of the Florida Everglades. From the icy little fishing ports of Alaska to the humid, Spanish moss-veiled bayous of Louisiana. From the crowded Fourth of July beaches of Coney Island or Atlantic City, New Jersey, to the almost deserted stretches of the Gulf of Mexico's Padre Island or the wind-swept sand dunes of the Outer Banks of North Carolina. From the huge expanses of Lake Superior, second largest in the world, to small sunny swimming holes found throughout the land. From quiet man-made Lake Mead spreading across the Arizona and Nevada deserts to the four million gallons of water per minute plunging over Niagara's American falls.

Each has its own attractions. Songsters harmonize about Suwannee, the Red River Valley, the wide Missouri. History buffs wander among the colonial settlements of the tidal James River, visit the restored seaport of Mystic, Connecticut or follow George Washington's footsteps to the Delaware or Potomac. Landscape painters remember Norman Rockwell's success and set up their easels at Rockport, Massachusetts. Escaping Manhattan executives hop on ferries bound for Fire Island; yachtsmen join the America's Cup race from the 'High Society' island of Newport, Rhode Island. Fishermen, perhaps with Hemingway in mind, head for the Deep Seas from the Florida Keys or for one of numerous thriving lakes and streams. Families establish themselves for a week-end or for a lifetime on one of the Thousand Islands floating in the St Lawrence or in one of the hundreds of residential areas and resorts found on the country's 88,633 miles of shoreland. Excursionists cruise up the Hudson gawking at the great cliff-side palaces built by American dukes of industry or paddle down the Mississippi on the *Delta Queen*. Canoeists glide in the sunset on mirror-calm lakes or, defying nature, transfer to kyacks or rubber rafts for death-defying plunges down rivers like the Colorado. Campers pitch their tents in state or national parks watered by geysers, falls, lakes and rivers.

With luck—if we preserve this great liquid heritage—most will discover, as did Mark Twain in *Life on the Mississippi* that 'The face of the water, in time, becomes a wonderful book—a book that was a dead language to the uneducated passenger, but which told its mind to me without reserve, delivering its most cherished secrets as clearly as if it uttered them with a voice.'

Left The sinuous Mississippi River coils ready to strike at the heartland of America. Here it is seen near its headwaters in Minnesota; 2,348 miles downstream it will pour into the Gulf of Mexico after draining 1,250,000 square miles in thirty-one states and two Canadian provinces.

Below Paddle wheel steamers of this type now found in Disneyland were a common sight on the Mississippi back when Mark Twain was a pilot on Old Man River. Now only one, the *Delta Queen*, regularly operates between Minnesota and New Orleans; others serve as restaurants or short excursion boats.

In only a few decades Honolulu's famed Waikiki Beach has changed from a sleepy, surf-side Shangri-la attracting only the wealthiest or the most adventuresome to a paradise for the package tourist. Multi-storey hotels tower above the palm trees; artificial pleasure gardens cover what once were swamps; Chinese, Japanese, mainland American and European restaurants compete with traditional Hawaiian lua for the attention of more than two million tourists; once-quiet streets and roads are choked with 400,000 automobiles; the rolling Pacific still sweeps in the surfers while sweeping out sixty million gallons of untreated sewage; often under-sensitive business-men praise the profits resulting from the tourist boom while sometimes over-sensitive environmentalists bewail the resulting pollution. The compromise – if and when it is found – will be watched closely, for America's fiftieth state and one of the New World's last New Frontiers could provide the crucible for a new formula to the tourist development of an increasingly affluent world.

Coney Island, New York City's biggest and most boisterous bath tub, may have changed many times since the first bath house was built in 1844 but it still attracts more than a million tourists on the Fourth of July alone. Gone are its 300 midgets, 32-acre Luna Park and the millionaires who used to dine in a restaurant shaped like an elephant; remaining are the best hot dogs in the world, the world's largest pleasure park wheel and a frolic in the Atlantic surf only forty minutes away from the concrete canyons of Manhattan.

Of all of America's coastal
cities, Miami Beach best
illustrates the supremacy
of man's mind over matter.
Until early this century
all of southern Florida
was what the Everglades
National Park's 1.5 million
acres still is today: a vast
wilderness of swamp, grass,
and mangrove and palm
trees (*above*). Then mid-
western automobile
millionaire Carl G. Fisher
saw its potential; using
money, men, machinery
and even a few elephants
he produced a golden sand
bar of seven square miles in
10 square miles of water.
Now some of Miami Beach's
more than three million
annual visitors choose to
return to the past: gliding
on boats through the
Everglades' great sea of
grass, sighting silent
Seminole Indians, corpse-
like alligators floating in
the sluggish water and
ghostly white egrets and
herons before returning to
the skyscraper hotels and
carefully manicured
beaches of the city.

Many of America's grand glacier-carved mountains are laced by waterfalls fed by the remaining glaciers and melting snow. Here the Hidden Falls gush down the steep slopes of Wyoming's Grand Teton National Park into Cascade Canyon. Among the world's most spectacular mountain landscapes because the view of its eastern slopes is unobscured by foothills, the Teton Range, rising in western Wyoming, derives its name from its tallest peak, the Grand Teton, piercing the clouds at 13,766 feet. Its purple snow-sprinkled pyramids are reflected in mirror lakes and in the twisting Snake River which coils at its feet; its large glacier debris-littered valley of Jackson Hole is a sanctuary for elk, bear and the rare trumpeter swan as well as for twentieth-century pioneers anxious to escape from the neon-lit world created by man to the sun-lit world created by nature.

Among the watery wonders of the world are North America's Niagara Falls (*above*) and the great natural fountains or geysers of Yellowstone National Park (*left*). Straddling the border between western New York and southern Ontario, the great Niagara cataract is split by Goat Island into the 165 feet high, 1,000 feet wide American Falls and the 155 feet high, 2,500 feet wide Canadian or Horseshoe Falls. About four million gallons of water per minute thunder over the lip of the American Falls into the Maid of the Mist Pool; even more drop over the Horseshoe Falls, providing an enormous source of hydroelectric power for both countries. The best-known of Yellowstone's fantastic geysers is, of course, Old Faithful, spewing 10,000 gallons of water as high as 180 feet in the air for four minutes faithfully every hour; here we see the Little Whirligig. The area in which they are found is the most extensive and spectacular of its kind in the world, encompassing 10,000 thermal springs! Not only is Yellowstone the oldest and one of the most popular of the U.S.'s National Parks, it is the largest, covering 3,472 square miles of Wyoming, Montana and Idaho.

Many of America's greatest cities have been created by the waters by which they stand. San Francisco (*left*) was a sleepy Spanish-Mexican mission settlement until gold was discovered 140 miles east in 1848. Then its bay became the Golden Gate for many of the 40,000 people who swarmed in to seek their fortune. At first, sailing ships choked the harbor and successful 'nobs' built gold-financed mansions on Nob Hill. After the gold rush, the city continued to attract trade and immigrants from the East. Rebuilt after the great earthquake and fire of 1906, San Francisco now has a population of 700,000 including at least 70,000 Chinese and 13,000 Japanese-Americans, its Embarcadero water-front area boasts more than forty deep water piers and its 46.6 square miles peninsula, bounded by the Pacific Ocean, the Golden Gate Strait and San Francisco Bay, is linked with the rest of the Bay Area by two famous bridges: the inspiring Golden Gate Bridge, and the Oakland Bay Bridge, (*seen here*) the longest (eight and a quarter miles) steel bridge in the world.

The long Pacific Coast of the United States varies greatly as it sweeps south from the rocky, sparsely populated promontories and coves of Washington and Oregon, past the charmingly utilized peninsula of San Francisco, down along the urban sprawl and sandy beaches of sunny southern California and then to Mexico. Here (*left*) Heceta Head light-house guards the wave- and wind-swept Oregon coast about 165 miles south of Portland. Standing on a cliff 249 feet above sea level and possessing a light which can be seen for twenty-six miles, the lighthouse and its promontory were named for Bruno Heceta, a Spanish explorer and the first European to see the mouth of the Columbia River (in 1775).

The face of many of the more arid areas of the United States has been completely changed by the large dams built in the first half of this century. Among them is one of the world's largest, the Hoover (*left*), formerly the Boulder Dam, completed in 1936 on the Arizona-Nevada border. The highest (726 feet) on the Colorado River, its 1,282-feet-long crescent top is a broad highway linking the two states washed by its waters. Lake Mead, which it formed, is the largest man-made lake in the U.S., covering 229 square miles and providing many recreational facilities as well as water power as far away as California.

New Harbor (*left*), with a
population of only a few
hundred, is typical of the
fishing villages found along
the coast of Maine. Nearly
as large as the five other
New England states
combined, the Pine Tree
State, as it is called because
of its great forests, has
2,400 miles of rocky, mist-
swept coastline, although
on the map it stretches only
250 miles north to south.
Its borders include the
eastern-most point of the
United States and many
islands, some of them
included in the ruggedly
beautiful Acadia National
Park which, among other
attractions, boasts the
highest elevation on the
coast. As with much of New
England, Maine's light-
house-guarded harbors and
coves have provided a
livelihood not only through
fishing and shipping but
through tourism.

The reflection of what is
most beautiful in America
is often found in its
thousands of serene,
woodland-surrounded
mirror lakes, such as Lake
Saranac (*right*) nestled in
upstate New York's
Adirondacks. Often
regarded as sacred by the
Indians, they still offer
sanctuary to those eager to
escape from the frenetic
pace of twentieth-century
urban America. Some lie
quiet and forgotten by all
but the most adventuresome
canoeists and hikers;
others are ringed by holiday
homes and filled with
happily splashing swim-
mers, water-skiers and
motor boaters; a few, sadly,
are filled with the debris of
a disposables-prone people.
Luckily, New York State
is particularly well endowed
with watery playgrounds,
encompassing within its
borders some 1,647 square
miles of water, including
800 miles of connecting
canals and rivers, hundreds
of lakes and ponds, the
Thousand Islands, boisterous Coney Island and quiet
mountain streams,
thunderous Niagara and a
lake known as Placid.

The sinuous Neches River (*below*) provides the outlet to the Gulf of Mexico for the oil refining and shipping interests of Beaumont, Texas. Easy outlets such as these have helped America's second largest state develop into one of its richest and most populous as well. On down the coast, Houston, fifty miles from the Gulf but linked by waterways, has become not only the oil capital of the nation and the most populous city in the south, but the sixth largest and one of the fastest growing cities in the land. Far from totally industrialized, the Texas Coast also includes the bare, beautiful beaches of Padre Island Seashore Park.

The shallow, sluggish waters of the Deep South have produced one of its most beautiful features, its mysterious Spanish-moss veiled cypress swamps and gardens. Some, such as Wilmington, North Carolina's Greenfield Gardens (*right*) have been tastefully landscaped for residents and tourists; others such as Georgia's Okefenokee Swamp, Mississippi's Pascagoula Swamp and Louisiana's bayou country remain steamy backwaters known only to cruising alligators, otters, muskrats and exotic birds. Many legends have developed around the gray moss which drapes not only these wild lands but also the plantation's avenues of live oaks. Perhaps the most romantic is the one which says it spread from the graying locks of a princess buried with her lover underneath these trees.

A solitary fisherman floating on a sunset-swept lake near Alexandria, Minnesota (*following pages*), typifies the serenity found by many Americans in the great waters of their land. Back in the huge cities and in the sprawling suburbs life may wash over them like a giant uncontrollable wave; here on this quiet lake in the state near where Hiawatha was supposed to live, it gently ebbs and flows and one can almost imagine Longfellow's young Indian brave 'in his birch canoe exulting'. Called 'The Land of Sky Blue Waters', Minnesota is particularly blessed: not only does it contain six per cent of the nation's total water supply and five of the country's largest lakes; 95 per cent of its population lives within five miles of recreational waters, its northern borders are washed by Lake Superior, largest fresh water lake in the world, and its center is watered by that Great Father of Waters, the Mississippi which has its source here.

MOUNTAINS, DESERTS, FORESTS AND PLAINS
The Body of the United States

O NLY ONE AMERICAN
mountain, Alaska's Mount McKinley, even makes the
list of the world's forty tallest—and that in thirty-ninth
place—and yet when we think of the United States of
America we think of soaring snow-capped peaks, of
great wall-like ranges, of 'purple mountains' majesty
above the fruited plains'.

Perhaps it is their presentation: rising
suddenly, dramatically from rippling oceans of grass;
encircled by sinuous rivers; reflected in clear mirror
lakes; decorated by garlands of alpine flowers and lacy
waterfalls; clothed in forests of giant and ancient trees;
crowned by shimmering caps of snow or by fierce vol-
canic haloes. Perhaps it's their simple but evocative
names: the Blue Ridge, the Alleghanies, the Ozarks, the
Rockies, the Sierra Nevada. Perhaps, their more bizarre
formations: weathered into domes, toadstools and skyscraper pinnacles by nature; sculpted into cliff-side
dwellings and historic monuments by man. Perhaps it's
their relationship to those early Americans who lived,
fought and died on their heights and in their shadows.

However, it is in the vast fertile flat-
lands that the secret of the American Dream really lies.
It is to them that the country owes its rapid economic and
population growth: the eastern coastal plain sweeping
like a scimitar down to Texas; to the Great Valley of
California; to the gentle, green, milk-producing fields
of the northeast and north-central; to the wind-swept
western and southwestern grasslands; to the miles and
miles of mid-western, river-irrigated heartland destined
to become one of the great cornucopias of the world.

In between these two extremes lie two
other extremes: the forests covering a third of the
country and contributing both to its economic health
and to the diversity of its domestic architecture, and the
great deserts and badlands, parched by unrelenting sun,
seamed with rich mineral and fuel deposits, split by
canyons so deep as to reveal a cross-section of the
country's geological history, decorated by huge cacti,
sagebrush and even an occasional mirage-like city,
guarded by grotesque freaks of nature's ill humor and
haunted by the ghosts of men, animals and towns aban-
doned here to die.

Even beyond these general extremes,
one can find specifics in this gigantic land encompassing
nine of the world's sixteen possible vegetational zones

The soaring, snow-capped,
mirror lake-reflected
mountains of Washington
State are among the most
inspiring in the country.
Known as the Cascades,
they run from north to
south through the west
central portion of the state,
including, not far from the
Canadian border, Mount
Shuksan (*right*). Described
as 'an area of alpine scenery
unmatched in the United
States', some 505,000 acres
were established by
Congress in 1968 as the
North Cascades National
Park.

and ten of its fourteen possible climates. There are mountains as high as Mount McKinley's 20,269 feet and deserts as low as Death Valley's 282 feet below sea level; flat-lands as fertile as Iowa's corn belt and as arid as Arizona's Painted Desert; trees as spectacular as the General Sherman sequoia towering 272 feet and measuring more than 35 feet at the base and as stunted as the wind-swept dwarfs on the Outer Banks of North Carolina; monuments as realistically carved by man as South Dakota's Mount Rushmore or as fantastically carved by nature as New Mexico's Carlsbad Caverns; states such as Alaska, large enough to encompass much of Europe or, such as Rhode Island, small enough to fit into less than half of the English county of Devon.

Sadly, today, much of this beauty lies outside our touch, imprisoned behind walls, barbed wire and 'no trespassing' signs. Luckily, although they have stopped short of Great Britain's humanitarian public footpath system, our private and governmental conservationists have provided us with the 2,000-mile-long Appalachian trail, the Blue Ridge Parkway and Skyline Drive, the thirty-five national parks encompassing some 46,000 square miles (or just over one per cent of the nation's total) and scores of scenic state and community preserves.

So we can still scale our country's tallest mountain, gaze into the depths of an active volcano's crater, wander through the bowels of mysterious limestone caverns, picnic among glaciers in alpine meadows, explore the Grand Canyon on muleback, glide through subtropical swamps, sun ourselves undeterred by property speculators on some, if not all, of America's loveliest beaches and imagine, with the narrator of *The Great Gatsby*, our pioneer ancestor, 'face to face for the last time in history with something commensurate to his capacity for wonder'.

The United States' 3,615,123 square miles include such extreme contrasts as Arizona's arid Painted Desert (*above*), Kansas's fertile plains and Alaska's sub-Arctic Mount McKinley. The rainbow-hued Painted Desert sweeps in a great crescent from the Grand Canyon southeast along the Little Colorado River to the Petrified Forest. The rolling Kansas plains which yielded two million buffalo hides between 1872–74 now yield agricultural produce for the farms of towns like Lindsborg (*above right*), known as 'Little Sweden, U.S.A.' because of the hundreds of Swedish immigrants who helped settle this area. Containing the exact center of the conterminous United States, Kansas was once the haunt of the wildest cowboys in the west, whose Bad Old Days are still relived every summer in Dodge City. Quite above such human folly is Mount McKinley (*right*), at 20,320 feet North America's highest mountain. Its national park has more than 3,000 square miles of starkly beautiful country, a sanctuary for moose, grizzly bears and 123 specie of bird, among them the magnificent golden eagle.

The red of wine and roses tints much of America's landscape from the fiery lava of Hawaii's volcanoes to Utah's pink and coral red sand dunes and the flesh of California's gigantic redwood trees. Luckily for nature lovers, all these scarlet ladies have been protected by the government in state and national parks. Visitors to 13,680 feet high Mauna Loa (*top*) and its less elevated but equally spectacular neighbor Kilauea in Hawaii's Volcanoes National Park can hike, ride, camp and study strange lava foundations, tropical flowers and bird life as well as watch the molten lava spurt from the glowing summits. Utah has protected its shifting, rosy-hued sand piles in Coral Dunes State Park south of Salt Lake City and near the Arizona border (*above*). But perhaps the most awe-inspiring natural wonders of all are the towering (as much as 300 feet high) redwoods (*right*), the tallest living things on earth. Found in the dim, sun-filtered cathedral-like atmosphere of Redwood National Park, they have incredible regenerative power, which is fortunate as their forests were being mowed down at an alarming speed until Congress created a preserve in 1968. These hardy monuments to nature's imagination may live anywhere from 400 to 2,500 years; even more awesome, they may be the descendants of trees standing 30 to 40 million years ago.

Nature's American paint box includes the cool, soothing blue and green tones of California's Lassen Volcano (*above*) and the hot, exciting ruby and golden tones of the area near Sedona, Arizona (*left*). Snow-capped Lassen, the largest plug dome volcano in the world, has rested serenely since its last eruption ceased more than a half century ago, settling into a strangely beautiful landscape setting of lava beds, cinder cones, mountain peaks, hot springs, lakes, steam vents and forests. Arizona, on the other hand, fires rather than cools the eye with its weird, sun-baked rock formations incorporating the remains of ancient oceans and swamps: dinosaur tracks, sharks' teeth, sea shells. The forty-eighth state to join the Union, it includes one of the country's greatest natural wonders, the Grand Canyon, and some of its fastest growing cities attracting people who prefer the natural canyons and skyscraper buttes of the west to the man-made ones of the north and east.

One of the world's leaders in preserving great natural wonders in national parks, the United States created its first and its largest in 1872. Today, Yellowstone's 3,472 square miles includes one of the country's most diversified assortments of scenic wonders including its breath-taking Grand Canyon and falls (*left*) as well as its better-known geysers and wildlife found throughout northwestern Wyoming and parts of Montana and Idaho.

Perhaps more than any other place in the country, Monument Valley (*above*) has contributed to our image of the Wild West. Although many of the most fabled events happened in less dramatic terrain—some even in the Midwest—it is here that we always find our John Ford heroes, racing on horseback through the surrealistic buttes and towers, pursued by bloodthirsty Indians. Carved by maddened elements from red sandstone, most of the valley is found in Arizona but part of it continues into Utah where, near the junction of the Colorado and Green Rivers, is also found Deadhorse Point (*following pages*), overlooking canyon grandeur rivaling that of Arizona's Grand Canyon.

One of the many western mountains attracting skiers is Oregon's 11,245-foot dormant volcano, Mount Hood (*above*) which can be seen towering above the surrounding forests from as far as eighty miles away. Near here passed explorers Lewis and Clark in 1805 en route to the Pacific; today's explorers skim down its ski runs, among them one of the world's longest, picnic in its flower-sprinkled alpine meadows and bike through its 1.1 million acres of forest.

Although not as dramatic as the majestic mountains beginning with the Rockies and extending further west to the Pacific coast, the older Appalachian system extending from Canada to Alabama has its own, less formidable allure. The great barrier which forced the early colonists to consolidate their culture rather than to spread it too thin on a premature migration west, the Appalachians include scenes such as these near Canaan in West Virginia (*right*) and at Grandfather Mountain near Linville, North Carolina (*right, top*). Once the mountain strongholds of pioneers, the remoteness of these hills encourages the perpetuation of many of the old customs and folk arts.

Most of the West's most spectacular scenery, such as Yosemite's Valley and waterfalls (*left*), were carved by nature; some, such as South Dakota's Mount Rushmore (*above*), were carved by man. But both Yosemite and Rushmore have at least one thing in common: Abraham Lincoln. Lincoln took the first step toward preserving for posterity what is now a 1,200 square miles national park by signing Yosemite into the care of California in 1864; his is also one of the four presidential faces carved on a Dakota mountainside by Gutzon Borglum, the others being Washington, Jefferson and Theodore Roosevelt. Cascading from a total height of 2,425 feet, the Yosemite Falls are the second highest in the world; Yosemite also boasts the High Sierras, groves of giant sequoias and clear lakes surrounded by alpine meadows. Rushmore is part of the Black Hills, an area which conjures up images of such legendary Old West characters as Calamity Jane and Wild Bill Hickok, and which also contains the 7,242-foot Harney Peak, highest North American mountain east of the Rockies.

In spite of earlier persecution, poverty and isolation the Indian tribes of the southwest have managed to survive and, in some cases, increase in such surprising and even hostile environments as the depths of Arizona's Grand Canyon (*left*) and Monument Valley (*below*). However, as remarkable as are the dwindling Havasupai living in a subtropical pocket of the Canyon, they are one of the least remarkable aspects of this great chasm which could swallow, almost without trace, the highest skyscrapers built by man. Up to eighteen miles wide, a mile deep and 217 miles long, the Canyon encompasses two billion years of geology and several different climates. All of it is the result of the determined Colorado River, first filing century after century down through the 300 million-year-old Redwall of Mississippian limestone, now cutting into black schists and pink granites so old they antedate life on Earth. The largest Indian tribe there, the Navajos, are to be found herding their sheep across the scrub land to the east of the Canyon in Arizona, spilling over into Utah. Once a war-like tribe which drifted down from

Canada in A.D. 1200–1400, they were subdued by Kit Carson in 1864. Many still live in the traditional way, sleeping and cooking in unhealthy dome-shaped hogans, dressing in nineteenth-century-style calico and velveteen garments and practising an early form of Women's Lib: the wife is the center of the family, owning and tending both flocks and crops and retaining the children in her clan; the man makes jewelry, tends to the horses and to the rituals and, increasingly, works for wages.

Untouched by the imprint of humanity, as is the scene (*left*) in Wyoming's Grand Teton National Park, or touched with a manifestation of the pioneering spirit of modern man, as is the scene in Washington's North Cascades National Park (*below*), the great mountain ranges of the United States remain an inspiration for an idealistic people. Here with his feet on high, firm ground but his head still out of the clouds, Man can obtain a new perspective of the land he and his ancestors have developed in the fertile plains, on the deserts, along the great waterways and throughout the cross-road towns and bustling cities thousands of feet below. Will it be a heritage he would bequeath as unchanged as possible to his children and grand-children or will he, in his own modest way, alter it, for better or for worse, even as the rains, ice and winds of centuries have altered the mountains on which he stands?

'WHAT MAKES A nation in the beginning is a good piece of geography,' poet Robert Frost said with customary common sense. The early settlers would doubtless have eventually agreed. Besides the great forests, teeming rivers and plains and rich soil already planted by the Indians with maize, potatoes and tobacco, they found themselves cradled in a natural nursery. To the east was the huge Atlantic Ocean discouraging all but the most disillusioned from returning home; to the west, the high barrier of the Appalachian Mountains, to north and south, dark forests inhabited by hostile savages.

So, rather than dissipating their strength wandering through wide open spaces as were the Spanish and French further west, they settled down in fortified villages, on farms and plantations, laying the foundations of the rural and village life which have contributed so much to twentieth-century nostalgia for the America of our past.

At first life was perilous. The earliest colony established in 1587 by Sir Walter Raleigh on what is now North Carolina's Roanoke Island disappeared, leaving only one trace: the Indian word 'Croatan' carved on a tree. Jamestown in Virginia endured Indian raids, a 'starving time', cruel diseases, internal quarrels, but survived by adopting a practical, democratic credo: no work, no food. In 1614, settler John Rolfe, husband of the Indian Princess Pocahontas, discovered the sweet-leaved variety of Indian tobacco which was to become the base of the colony's economy. In 1619 each freeman was granted 100 acres of land; the first Negro slaves were imported by a Dutch ship and ninety brides were eagerly bid for by woman-hungry settlers. Soon 700 or so settlers were scattered along a seventy-mile strip on the edge of the wild new continent, and the plantation system was born. At first, they clung to the shores of rivers like the James, producing tobacco and landed gentry in spite of bloody Indian massacres; later they spread to the flat, humid lands of the Deep South, producing cotton, rice and indigo and an overblown way of life almost destined to go with the wind.

Even as the South remained an agrarian society with small sleepy Spanish-moss-draped towns and no large cities except Charleston, South Carolina, the North developed in a quite different direction. Neat, bustling, mercantile towns grew up

One of the great riches of the United States is its vast, flat, fertile farmlands. Sometimes they are found sweeping away to the horizon without a tree, person or mountain in sight. Other times they are found coiling like a plump, multi-striped green or golden snake through foothills and forests, their lushness possibly even contrasted with the stark skyscraper or smoke-stack skyline of a nearby metropolis. It is difficult to believe, for instance, that this harmonious abstract agricultural pattern (*right*) is found in Pennsylvania, third most populous state of the nation and site of such large and/or industrialized cities as Philadelphia, Pittsburgh and Bethlehem. Yet, still the state remains true to the meaning of its name – Penn's woods – for approximately half of it is woodland and much of the rest is quiet rolling countryside marked by neat white fences and farmhouses.

around the symbols of Puritan life: the simple white frame or brick churches, their spires pointing upwards as a reminder of the heavenly rewards to come for those combining godliness with industry. Farms were small and efficiently run; the emphasis was on variety rather than one crop, on hard personal endeavor rather than on the overseeing of slave labor; the unit of government was the township not the county.

Between the geographical and cultural extremes of New England and the South grew up the Middle Colonies, tolerant, cosmopolitan and destined to develop some of the country's first great cities. Behind them all was the frontier, breeding tough men capable of fighting, or trading with, the Indians, intrepid women able to produce from a forest clearing and a log cabin a way of life still found today in the mountain strongholds of Appalachia.

Then one of these mountain men, Daniel Boone, blazed a path through the mountains and the rush was on. By the time of the War for Independence a half million settlers were on the frontiers, building homes, schools, churches and roads, dividing the fertile, river-watered flatlands into a checker-board of territories, shoving the Indians off their lands, establishing the occasional market or transport town along the watery highways of the Great Lakes or Mississippi.

Some of these towns were to develop into great cities; others such as Ste. Genevieve, Missouri, and Natchez, Mississippi, became museums of ornate antebellum architecture; still others such as Hannibal, Missouri, and Sauk Centre, Minnesota, inspired authors such as Mark Twain and Sinclair Lewis to fictionalize the charms and defects of small town America. The land around developed, according to its geography and climate, into rippling fields of red wheat grown from grains brought from the Russian steppes, into coal and oil industrial areas, into vast acreages of corn 'as high as an elephant's eye', into rolling green dairy land producing, among other products, delicious Wisconsin cheeses. By 1830 more than half the Americans had been brought up in this new atmosphere, far from the government centers of the East. Then a new frontier opened up: the United States annexed the former Mexican territories of Texas, Arizona, Nevada, California and Utah.

Although some of the Forty-niners who rushed to California for gold stayed to irrigate and farm its valleys, the real impetus for settlement came from the Mormons, the cowboys and sheep farmers and the homesteaders. At first the herdsmen wandered at will; the fields were verdant with grain; the mines yielded gold and silver. Then the cowboys found themselves fenced in–or out–by the settlers' barbed wire, droughts struck, finally producing in the 1930s the great disaster recorded by John Steinbeck in *The Grapes of Wrath*, the small mines played out leaving skeletal workings and empty, ghost-haunted towns. Now the West is a region of dramatic contrasts: wind-swept towns where they long since saw the last picture show– and the frenetic neon-lit oasis of Las Vegas; the sprawling ranch-house suburbs of Los Angeles–and the vast

ranches producing the thirty-nine million head of cattle and ten million sheep annually slaughtered in the United States; the dramatically bleak canyons and deserts of Arizona, Utah and New Mexico–and the rich, irrigated orchards and vineyards of California.

Even the next frontier–the Hawaiian islands–was soon to find its rural areas dotted with pineapple plantations; its towns and villages filled with tourists. Only Alaska remains to be exploited by the oilmen, explored by the tourists, its fishing villages not drastically changed by statehood.

For the fact is that America has changed more than we realize. When those of us over 50 were born, half the population was rural; when those of us under 25 were born, two-thirds was metropolitan. We still think of ourselves romantically as a nation of small-town folk and farmers, yet most small towns have become cities, suburbs or crumbled into obscurity and only five per cent of our population is actually farming the land. By the year 2000, 85 per cent of the descendants of explorers and plantation owners, homesteaders and cowboys will live in metropolitan areas. Who could have guessed it when Thomas Jefferson made his Louisiana Purchase, when Daniel Boone struggled through the mountains, when Lewis and Clark stood on the Rockies scanning a great, uninhabited land?

Just waiting for Thanksgiving are these hundreds of turkeys in a California mass-production poultry plant. The most American of domestic fowls, they are natives of North America. Explorers in the sixteenth century found them domesticated in Central America and Mexico and American colonists found them one more reason for gratitude during their first Thanksgiving prayers.

This typical Middle American small town crossroads scene is found, appropriately enough, in Indiana, 'The Crossroads of America'. Located in a rolling area filled with tobacco, grain and vegetable farms efficiently run by friendly Hoosiers, it is a scene that is all too rapidly disappearing from the American landscape as more and more people move from villages and towns into the sprawling suburbs of the great metropolises.

The early New England colonists settled in small villages clustered around immaculate white churches, center of their theocratic way of life and similar to Waits River in central Vermont (*above*). Soon after the Revolutionary War, however, their hardy Green Mountain boys and other pioneers were over the mountains and into the plains beyond, taking with them the concept of the one-family farm or homestead. The enormity of the plains, and three inventions, soon persuaded them to think big and literally and figuratively to sow the seeds which have turned the Midwest in general and states like Illinois (*following pages*) in particular into the mass-production breadbasket of the nation and much of the world. The first invention was the heavy-duty plow invented by Vermont-born Illinois resident, John Deere; the second was the mechanical reaper invented by the young Virginian, Cyrus McCormick, the forerunner of the huge reapers (*right*) which today harvest the thousands of miles of golden Midwestern grain; and the third was barbed wire, which helped protect the farmers' new fields from the sheep and cattle of itinerate shepherds and cowboys.

Even as some of America's history died in the making, leaving behind only its shell in such spots as the mining ghost town of Telluride, Colorado (*above*), other history lives and thrives as in the neat farms of the Pennsylvania Dutch (*left*), who manage to make a living while retaining the customs and religion of their forefathers. Between 1840 and 1866, two and a half million people rushed into Colorado in search of silver and gold. Some of their boom towns turned into thriving Rocky Mountain cities such as Denver; others have turned into museum pieces attracting tourists to the garish old hotels, noisy saloons or even an opulent opera house built by the gold dust of spendthrift miners; most, such as Telluride, population 677, support a handful of hangers-on or crumble peacefully into obscurity. Meanwhile the Pennsylvania Dutch, actually members of various German-origin or deutsch religious sects, continue to go about Their Father's business, dressed in dull fashions from a by-gone age, traveling in horse-drawn buggies and farming their pretty, rolling farmlands, in as non-mechanized a way as possible.

Eighty-five per cent of the pineapple juice and sixty-five per cent of the canned pineapple consumed annually by the American people comes from our only island state, Hawaii. In turn, the ground-growing fruit seen on the conveyor belt (*left*) brings nearly $150 million into the fiftieth state, an amount topped only by its sugar production. One whole island, Lanai, is completely owned by one of the largest pineapple growing and canning firms. Other exports from the fertile islands include coffee, papaya, macadamia nuts, guava nectar, passion fruit juice and a variety of exotic flowers.

Above State, county and local fairs with their prize bulls, homemade pies, merry-go-rounds and bizarre sideshows are as American as Thanksgiving or the Fourth of July. Ohio alone has as many as a hundred county fairs; among its better-known events is the Circleville Pumpkin Show in Pickaway County, famous for those big orange things Americans traditionally place in the windows on Halloween night.

'He went thataway' and 'Going, going, going for a song', are two refrains frequently heard in small-town America. Either martyred or maligned by films and television, the small-town cop is usually more of an official busybody than either a hero or a villain. At his best he's the warm, humane guardian and friend of the community –young and old, black and white; at his worst, he's the uniformed epitome of its small-town, small-minded bile and bigotry. As for the auctions, a lot of things get left behind in a mobile society such as ours (47 per cent of our population moved to new homes between 1965–1970 says the most recent census). Often they are junk, sometimes they are a real treasure: an old Victorian rocker from a New England farmhouse; a 300-year-old rosewood table from a Southern mansion, the diary of an early settler, or a beautiful rainbow-hued quilt carefully made by hand by a Kentucky mountain woman.

We may be One Nation
Under God, but never has
any nation had so many
ways of worshipping its
God, from a simple red
brick Christian church
(*above*) in Deal, New Jersey,
to an ornate Buddhist
temple in Hawaii; from a
spartan Presbyterian
service in Ossining, New
York (*right*) to a lavish
Jewish wedding in Holly-
wood, California; from a
spontaneous Bible-
thumping, foot-tapping
Georgia Baptist tent-revival
to a 375-voice, 11,000 pipe,
voice and organ concert in
Salt Lake City's Mormon
Tabernacle. Yet another
American freedom: to
worship as we please.

Almost every small town
has its band, its parades,
its majorettes doing their
thing with flaming batons
as they strut down Main
Street. Here, the high
school band of Millersburg,
Ohio (population 2,982)
plays in the town square
for the annual antiques fair.

This neat, proudly maintained farm near de Kalb, Illinois (*above*), is typical of those found throughout the state which has been called 'an island prairie through which the heartland pumps its produce'. Scenes like this make some of us nostalgic for the rural America of the early 1900s when sixty per cent of our population lived in a farm and small town environment. Today, that percentage has changed to only twenty-six and the actual farmers, farm workers and their families account for only five per cent of our population! Still the vast fertile farmlands of our Midwest remain, farmed in a new and more efficient way, feeding our people and millions of others around the world.

Ever since oil was discovered in Oklahoma in 1920, oil wells like this one (*below*) have become a common sight throughout the flat rolling former cowboy country. However, it still has not forgotten its earlier days: Oklahoma City boasts the National Cowboy Hall of Fame and one third of the total Indian population of America, some sixty-seven tribes, reside in the state.

The irrigated truck farming areas of California have been made famous in the fiction of John Steinbeck. Here is the fact (*right*); hot, tiring work done by Japanese-American farm-hands near Ventura. The third largest state in size and the first in population, California has great physical and agricultural variety: from rugged mountains to vast desert, from vineyards producing some of the best wines in America to all the ingredients for the best chef's salad in the land.

Above 'Ride em, cowboy' is still the cry at rodeos held throughout the southwest and northeast of the United States. The cowboy may have been forced to turn into a rancher with the influx of homesteaders and the advent of barbed wire fences during the last century, but his skills of bronco busting, steer riding and rope-handling still pull the crowds as do the dude ranches, historical re-enactments and Wild West towns found through-out the great flat lands of North America.

Right Some of the most renowned thoroughbred-horse-rearing farms of the world are to be found among the tender Blue Grass fields surrounding Lexington, Kentucky. Not only do they export some of the world's most famous race horses, they import tourists who visit the stud farms, attend the annual May Kentucky Derby at Louisville's Churchill Downs or the August State Fair Horse Show or even bid for a yearling at the July or September auctions.

THE AMERICAN PEOPLE
The Soul of a Many-Headed Nation

'WHAT, THEN, IS the American, this new man?' French settler Hector St John Crêvecoeur asked early in the history of our new republic, anticipating the question we–and others–still ask today.

It was a question easier to answer then at the dawn of our independence than now at the dawn of our third century as a nation. Crêvecoeur's Americans had been, until that point, at least technically Europeans. Their past had been put behind them with their crossing of the Atlantic; their future lay like a new and empty slate waiting to be filled. Their geographical, economic and political horizons were as wide and un-cluttered as the vast landscape stretching away to the unsettled west. Their aspirations for the most part were single-minded: to carve a new life, and perhaps wealth, from a virgin country. Their spirit was exhilarated–after all, they had just defeated one of the world's great powers; their minds, in the words of Crêvecoeur, were occupied by 'those new thoughts which mark an American'.

Today the thoughts and actions of the American people are the subject of national and international psychoanalysis. Our fans, and they are legion, are impressed by our hospitality, our warmth, our shrewdness, our creativity, our zest for both work and play, our resourcefulness, our classlessness, our business acumen, our flamboyance, our self-reliance, our generosity, our inventiveness, our idealism, our vibrant if sometimes faulted democracy, our efforts, in spite of the adverse aspects of human nature, to build a successful, multi-racial, multi-cultural society.

Who else, they will say, could produce the world's most breathtaking skyscrapers and small folksy towns with signs at the city limits urging 'Now Ya'll Hurry Back'; Leonard Bernstein and Fats Domino; Woodrow Wilson and Teddy Roosevelt; the dry martini and Prohibition; hot dogs and a champagne breakfast at Brennans; the Wright Brothers and the Marx Brothers; Jackson Pollock and Norman Rockwell; Mae West and Cary Nation; Ford assembly lines and New England country stores; the Marshall Plan–not to mention the Peace Corps–and one of the most internationally competitive business communities in the world.

With a tragic irony, the first black Americans arrived on a Dutch slave ship the same year, 1619, and the same place, Jamestown, Virginia, as the first assembly of popular government in America. In the more than three and a half centuries since, the descendants of those first twenty slaves and the thousands of other Africans forcibly brought to our country, have multiplied to more than twenty million black citizens; meanwhile our democracy has continued to proclaim that 'all men were created equal' while denying, at least until recently, the most basic rights of those who could, in some cases, trace their American ancestry back beyond that of some Daughters of the American Revolution. At first the struggle for Civil Rights began in the Deep South where this African American (*right*) is seen enjoying an outdoor concert of Afro-America's most internationally famous art form, jazz; more recently it has migrated with the deprived, under-educated southern rural blacks to the huge, industrialized cities of the north.

Our detractors, on the other hand, accuse us of being unattractively materialistic, politically naive in some of our foreign policies, politically hypocritical in some of our domestic policies—publicly taking an idealistic stance, privately following the dictates of everything from questionable big businessmen to rifle association lobbies—and prone to violence, racialism and extremism.

To find out what we are we must rediscover what we were. From colonial to modern times many of our settlers came to America because they were deprived of money, rank, status and/or property as well as of freedom in the countries they left behind. Hard work and democratic cooperation, they soon discovered, proved almost mandatory for survival. Out of this grew our present insistence upon democracy and free enterprise, our glorification, almost deification of work and economic success; our advocacy of religious freedom even while attempting to superimpose our moral values on others in the community.

Of course geography played its part, molding the conflicting cultures and personalities of North and South, producing racial and political problems still disturbing our country today. Then, as the pioneers moved further inland, two other apparently conflicting patterns became woven into American life: its neighborliness and its violence. The first was the almost inevitable result of a life where one's neighbor was often the sole support against disaster. The second had more complex origins: the determination of early settlers not to be deprived of their weapons resulting in today's belief that it is every citizen's right to be armed regardless of his motives; the imported blood codes of some immigrant groups; the obsession with obtaining and protecting property; the lawlessness of the west, the slaughter of the Indians and the institution of slavery. As Alexis de Tocqueville wrote in 1831 after visiting Kentucky and Tennessee slave owners, 'the habit of uninhibited command gives men a certain feeling of superiority which makes them impatient of opposition and irritated at the sight of obstacles.'

The great surge westward led to other influences on our society today: rootlessness as we continue to search for new frontiers; adaptability as we find them and inventiveness as we manufacture the means of tailoring them to our dreams. With the huge influx of Irish, German, Polish, Scandinavian, Chinese and other immigrants in the middle of the last century came other contributions still seen in our way of life: new loyalties and values; new forms of food—bagels, pizza, chop suey, borscht, goulash; new urban and industrial problems and, inevitably, new forms of political manipulation as city 'machines' and 'bosses' preyed upon the insecurity, language difficulties and national loyalties of the new Americans as well as upon the prejudices of the old. On the surface it would appear that their differences have been melted away. Then comes New York City's St Patrick's Day Parade, San Francisco's Chinese New Year, a Puerto-Rican-Black gang fight, the World War II incarceration of Japanese Americans, a pro- or anti-Zionist rally by former Eastern Europeans or a sud-

denly overheard blues refrain from the black descendant of a Mississippi slave. Even our first settlers, the Indians, no longer remain silent, forcing us to face the hypocrisy of some of our ideals as compared to painful reality.

This is a reality already faced by many of our most creative playwrights and novelists and by some of our more conscientious political figures. Perhaps our aims have been too Messianic, our desires too materialistic, our motives too conflicting. Yet we've evolved into a remarkable People: a nation constantly interested in bettering itself not just materialistically but through education and self-knowledge; a country truly concerned about the plight of others in the world; a mixture of cultures on the whole sincerely attempting to live in harmony. As long as we continue to question, probe, seek and democratically find new and better solutions to the basic emotional, spiritual, political and economic needs of our personal and national life; as long as we retain a sense of perspective about present events as well as a sense of pride in the past; as long as we realize that the American Dream should be something distilled from our own spirit rather than bottled and sold by political and economic alchemists; as long as we understand that new frontiers need neither be geographical nor materialistic, then we can believe we can become, in the nineteenth-century prediction of Madame de Staël, 'the advance guard of the human race'.

Two of the United States' most multi-racial cities are Honolulu and San Francisco. Everyone in the Hawaiian islands is a member of an ethnic minority, no single racial group constitutes more than about one third of the population, and since World War II, one out of three marriages have been inter-racial. The original,

Polynesian population is represented (*above left*) by this attractive Honolulu maiden making welcoming flower leis for the tourists. As for San Francisco, some 150,000 of its residents are of Italian extraction, like the gregarious seafood salesman (*above*) seen on the city's famous Fisher-man's Wharf. In its picturesque Chinatown,

San Francisco has the largest Chinese settlement outside of Asia with some 70,000 residents, while its 'Little Japan' caters to some 13,000 Japanese-American residents. The diversity of its other ethnic groups is proved by the existence of some twenty-three foreign language newspapers.

Of America's many ethnic groups, perhaps the most determined to retain their traditions are Pennsylvania's frugal Amish (*left*), who are of German extraction. Wearing long beards or dresses, covering themselves in somber covers and disdaining such new-fangled contraptions as automobiles, they remain close to God and nature in a landscape of rolling farmlands and neat white-walled farmhouses and barns. Long considered an anachronism, they take on a new significance in a world increasingly polluted by mechanism and urbanization.

For perhaps as long as 1,200 years, wave after wave of inter-Pacific immigration has landed on the shores of Hawaii, America's fiftieth and only island state. Among the more recent migrations has been one from the Philippines, represented by the German-Filipino-American beauty (*below*) being admired on a Honolulu beach by another multi-racial American passer-by.

Although the sturdy Texas cowboys seen here (*right*) may well be of Anglo Saxon-American extraction, much of their traditional way of life and many of their words—ranch, patio, lasso, chaps, bronco came from the Spanish conquistadors who introduced both the horse and the cow to America.

Nobody is sure exactly how and when the original Americans, the American Indians, arrived but it is generally agreed that they came from Asia, which would explain the proud Oriental features of this young Crow boy (*right*), that they passed over a no-longer existent bridge of land from Siberia to Alaska and that they arrived no later than 15,000 years ago. Long one of the country's most neglected, if sometimes stubbornly isolationist, minorities, today some are found in tiny, fertile farming reservations or in huge—in the case of the Navajos, larger than Costa Rica—arid reservations, while others have become part of the mainstream American society. Many are proud of their heritage and participate regularly in tribal festivals; the young Crow, for instance, was photographed at one of the best known, the annual Gallup, New Mexico, Inter-Tribal Indian Ceremonial. Meanwhile the country has apparently been able more easily to assimilate more recent Asian arrivals, though they often prefer to reside in Chinese communities such as New York's Chinatown (*below*) where they can retain their own architecture, customs, religion and festivals.

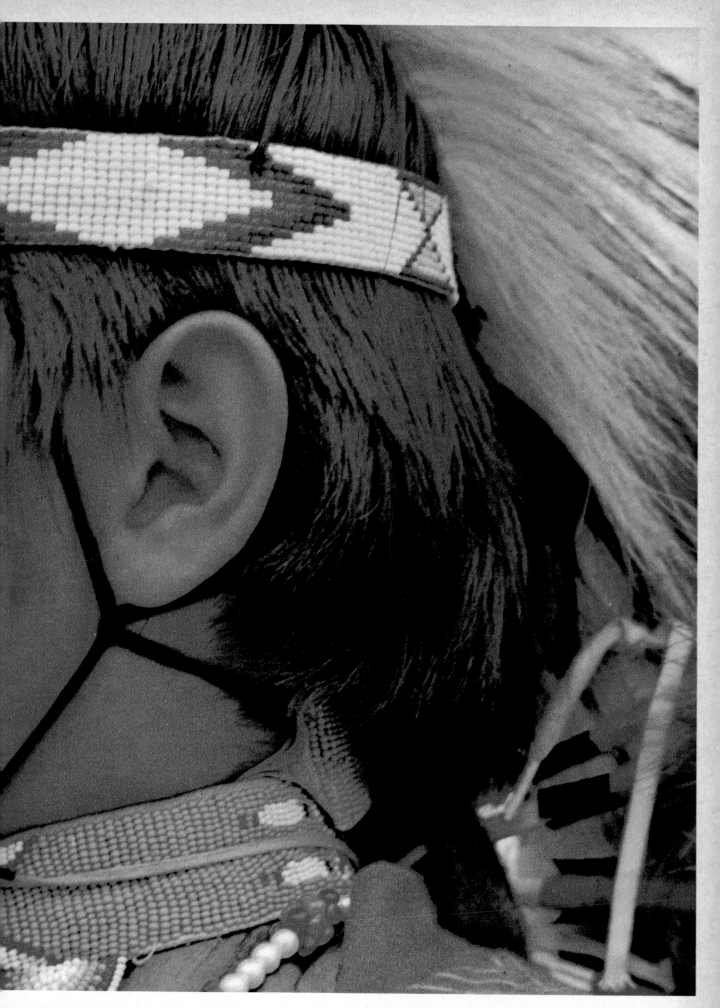

Our multi-culture, multi-racial society has produced not only one of the most exciting progressive cultures in the world but frustrations and problems which have become particularly obvious in our largest, most over-crowded cities. Faced by these problems–creeping slums, racialism, juvenile delinquency, violence and drugs–many city dwellers have taken the time-honored American way out: they have moved on, this time to suburbs which themselves have sometimes evolved into sub-cities with the very same problems. Others have taken an equally traditional American stance: they have stayed put to fight for a better life for themselves and their children. Here (*left* and *top right*) the March on Drugs advises fellow New Yorkers to 'Get High on Life' rather than buy the drugs peddled first by the Mafia, an Italian-American criminal minority, and now increasingly by black and Puerto Rican gangsters. In fact, public protest has become more and more part of the American way of life during the past decade or so, partly because of a constructive desire to stand up publicly and be counted, partly because of an alarming disillusionment with the calmer, more methodical means of change through elected, representative government.

Be they residents of the smallest town or the largest metropolis, all Americans love a parade. Sometimes it's actually a demonstration, a protest about some problem; more often it's just exuberance: a sense of fun or fantasy, or pride or patriotism. It may be a group of small, neatly uniformed Girl Scouts or a group of large, dishevelled Irish-Americans celebrating St Patrick's Day in the traditional way: with a lot of beer and as much sentiment. It may honor an Hawaiian king, as does Honolulu's Kamehameha Day procession, or an Afro-American jazz musician, as does many a boisterous New Orleans funeral procession. It may be scheduled by a seasonal, sporting, or historic event such as St Paul, Minnesota's Winter Carnival, Miami's Orange Bowl Festival or Cheyenne, Wyoming's Frontier Days. Its costumes may range from the tiniest bikinis worn by the local beauty queens to the elaborate plumed costumes of New Orleans' Mardi Gras Indians or Philadelphia's Mummers. There is almost always a galaxy of strutting majorettes (perhaps even whirling flaming batons), costumed representatives of local fraternal orders, a convoy of elaborate floats and, of course, at least one booming brass band.

Novelists, film and television producers, journalists and just the average American have always been alternatively attracted and repulsed by the American policeman. On the one hand, he has been seen as the friendly, foot-sore neighborhood cop prepared to risk his dignity or even life to protect people or property. On the other hand, he has been seen as corrupt, violent and racist; prepared, for instance, to set dogs and fire hoses against Alabama Negro demonstrators or tear gas and truncheons against protestors at a Chicago political convention. In the mind of one American film fanatic he may be the slow, gum-chewing but ultimately noble Southern cop of 'The Heat of the Night'; to another, a clever but unorthodox 'Dirty Harry' to a third, a tough 'New Centurion'. The truth, of course, lies well between the extremes just as the role of a policeman varies depending upon whether he's a motor-cycle-riding sheriff of the super highways as the Los Angeles traffic policeman (*left*) or a small-town foot soldier on first-name basis with all along his beat.

One man, one vote has always been one of the most fervent, if sometimes perverted, beliefs of American democracy. Beginning with the early settlers who held the first legislative council in a Jamestown, Virginia, church in 1619 and who signed the Mayflower Compact the following year, the system has evolved to encompass the New England town meeting, the Constitution of the United States, the establishment of a two-house Congress providing states both with equal votes and with votes based upon population, the Lincoln-Douglas debates, the circus-like national political conventions, the federal protection of Black voters terrorized by southern racialists and, most recently, the nationwide Watergate court cases produced by the realization that men not elected by our votes but in positions of power were influencing the policies of our country. Behind all this, however, is a nation aware, as one eighteenth-century Constitutional Convention delegate put it, that frequent elections are 'the only defense of the people against tyranny', and individuals prepared, like the New York State candidate (*above*) to serve their country as spokesmen for fellow voters or to campaign on New York City's 5th Avenue (*below*) for voter registration.

'The business of America is business,' President Calvin Coolidge said in his usual terse manner some fifty years ago. Times haven't changed in spite of the more relaxed philosophies of our various alternative societies; business success is still a powerful American stimulus, be it the business of building a bigger and better Manhattan sky-scraper (*left*) or the business of producing a smaller and more efficient mousetrap in Minneapolis. From the brisk, efficient New England country store owner to the founder of, for instance, a grocery store chain, we remain the wonder of much of the rest of the world: not only do we work hard and generally efficiently, we actually seem to enjoy our work. Part of our impetus came from our colonial heritage: 'no work, no food,' Governor Thomas Dale decreed to the first Virginia settlers. Then there was the impetus for invention among a new nation faced with unusual problems: both Thomas Jefferson and Benjamin Franklin met the challenge as did many an unsung pioneer faced with a new type of soil, the problem of how to build a plains house without wood, the need for a new, better hunting knife. The New World's vast distances, great agricultural and mining potential, powerful forms of energy and human resources, inspired new, time-saving, mass production businesses of communication, trans-portation, farming, meat and dairy production and mining and industrial technology. The negative results of our free enterprise, big business society have produced criticism throughout the world. But the positive results are the envy of the world: one of the highest living standards ever known; a classless appreciation of the working man; an encouragement of imagination, invention, self-reliance and efficiency; an ability not only to invent but quickly to mass-produce new products; a pride in our work, be it designing skyscrapers or kitchen sinks, selling dresses in the rag trade or space suits to the government.

Not only do we work hard, we play hard. Sometimes it is at a barbecue in our own back yard, at a Little League baseball game, or at a local festival like the New Orleans Jazz Festival where this young musician (*left*) is shown blowing his heart out for his church jazz and gospel band. But increas-ingly it is away from home. Some places, like Las Vegas and Miami Beach, keep us firmly in the twentieth century, while others, such as the reconstructed ghost towns of the West or the reconstructed Early American villages of the East take us back into a less complicated past. A growing number whisk us away into the Fantasy World of Peter Pan. Thus at Disneyland (*below*) one can be figuratively carried away by a costumed balloon seller or literally carried away by a 'Life on the Mississippi' paddleboat steamer.

More than perhaps any other people in the world Americans love dressing up and re-creating or perpetuating the customs of the past. Four times a year muzzle-loading rifle buffs dressed in suitable pioneer costume (*left*) gather in Indiana to compete in target shoots and tomahawk-throwing contests. Once a year Wyoming, where more than a million head of cattle still roam, plays host to real cowboys and girls and rodeo stars (*right*) as well as to tourists anxious to savor, if only for a few days, the Wild West at Cheyenne's Frontier Days. But they are only two examples of a national love of historic pageantry. On any one day, one might find a modern Scarlet O'Hara complete with honeyed drawl and hoop skirts sweeping across the lawns of a South Carolina plantation, her colonial counterpart in mob-cap and farthingale giving historical lectures in a Williamsburg, Virginia mansion or a Mystic, Connecticut, sea captain's house, or one of their menfolk, perhaps a baker or banker by profession, camping out in Revolutionary War uniform on a Saratoga, New York, battlefield. Then there are the stately home tours, the mock Wild West gun battles, the literally hundreds of history- and costume-inspired festivals and, of course, the great historic dramas in which one might find Cherokee Indians portraying their ancestors' tragic forced migration, a Virginia businessman portraying Thomas Jefferson or even a North Carolina infant portraying Virginia Dare, the first child born in North America of English parents.

Be they geared to amateurs or professionals, spectators or participants, sports add to the variety of American life. Joe DiMaggio, Joe Namuth, Muhammad Ali are only a few of the American heroes produced by our favorite leisure-time activities. The Harlem Globe Trotters, various tennis and golfing stars, the Kentucky Derby and the Indianapolis 500 are known in parts of the world that consider American baseball and football as peculiar as we consider cricket and bull fighting. But perhaps our biggest thrill can come from watching a university team at a match, such as this one between the University of Oklahoma and Oklahoma State (*top*), or check-mating one's opponent in a chess match in New York's Greenwich Village (*above*), or hitting one's first home run in a baseball game, such as this one at Malibu Beach, California (*right*).

Americans are unusually lucky in the variety and beauty of their country. From quiet fishing pools like this one in South Dakota, to roaring 'white water' torrents challenging the most skillful canoeists; from the snow-covered ski slopes of Sun Valley, Idaho, to the sunny beaches of Sea Island, Georgia; from the dude ranches of Montana and Wyoming to the cypress gardens of South Carolina and Florida; from the rain forests of Washington State to the deserts of Nevada; from the lush semitropical gardens of Hawaii to the icy slopes of Alaska – Americans have an opportunity afforded few people to utilize their leisure time in landscapes of true magnificence. Perhaps this is why we remain a nation of part-time pioneers. We fish much as Hiawatha did on deep, ripple-less lakes, camp in quiet forest glades seldom seen by man, wade in tidal New England pools, swim in clear mountain rivers, hunt the moose, the bear or the deer in wildernesses once known only to American Indians, and ride on horseback across the great plains, as did the early Spanish conquistadors.

AMERICA'S GREAT cities are the most conspicuous monuments to the virtues and vices of the land from which they have sprung.

Their urban cliff dwellings and sprawling suburbs have gradually and rather surprisingly absorbed 71 per cent of our people–from millionaires to migratory farmers, from the descendants of their founding fathers to non-English-speaking immigrants; their vitality has injected spirit into creative souls stifled by the small towns and rural communities from which they have fled; their huge industrial complexes have developed into the computerized cornucopias of a western consumer society; their glittering steel and glass towers have become as much symbols of the New World's desire literally and figuratively to rise above the old as were Egyptian pyramids, Grecian temples, Italian palaces and German castles in their time; their city halls and universities, film studios and art galleries have held a mirror up to the problems which may soon become common around our rapidly urbanizing globe.

For here in the caldrons of our canyon cities the problems of the megalopolis have somehow come more quickly to the boil, thus one finds in New York City one of the country's first great central urban parks and a public frightened to use it; in San Francisco, the great inspiring sweep of the Golden Gate Bridge and disillusioned youths using it only as a launching pad to eternity; in Detroit, the great automobile factories which have helped create a suburban nation and a city center which has rapidly deteriorated as thousands of residents–120,000 in three years–fled to its all-white suburbs; in Washington, the stirring white marble monuments to the founders of our democracy and the depressing black slums testifying to one of its unforeseen realities.

Certainly, that great advocate of agrarian democracy, Thomas Jefferson, could not have foreseen that one of our cities, Detroit, would have more murders in one year than Belfast, Ireland in four and a half years of civil strife, when he wrote to an acquaintance in 1800, 'I view great cities as penitential to the morals, the health and the liberties of man.'

Nor could William Penn envisage that his 'green country town' of Philadelphia would produce some of the New World's first exclusive suburbs from

New York City stands tall, tough, glittering –proud to be the largest city in the United States of America and one of the largest in the world. Her heart is in Manhattan, her pulse is the throbbing of traffic, the push of a rush-hour crowd, the tempo of a jazz band. Her arteries run scarlet and royal blue, golden and green with the life blood of neon. Her mind is on Broadway and in a half dozen museums. Her stomach is for the rag trade and Madison Avenue, for transportation and television, for finance and tourism. But her soul is in her nearly eight million residents. The first settlers arrived from the Netherlands in 1626; now the city has sixteen million visitors annually from all parts of the world. They stand on the top of the Empire State Building–now topped in height by the World Trade Towers–marveling at the man-made peaks and canyons in panorama before them. They browse in almost medieval calm through the Cloisters Museum or join the crowd watching the hysterical, gesticulating mobs on the floor of the New York Stock Exchange. They have coffee in a bohemian Greenwich Village shop, eat at leisure in one of the world's most expensive restaurants or grab a quick pizza in what may be the world's only Yiddish Pizza Parlor. They pay to see an amusing show on Broadway, off-Broadway or off-off-Broadway or just watch it for free in a cafe, on a street-corner, in a park or anywhere else where two or more New York 'characters' are likely to assemble.

1870 along the excellent Main Line train service of the Pennsylvania Railroad.

Even that most visionary of visitors, Alexis de Tocqueville, probably didn't look in his crystal ball in 1831 to discover 'that pretty town', Boston, becoming part of a huge east coast urban sprawl expected, along with its California counterpart, to encompass 54 per cent of our population by the year 2000.

America's early history contributed not only to the common problems but to the tremendous differences in its great twentieth-century cities. When the first settlers arrived they had a spirit of community as well as a need, for security reasons, to cluster around the mainstays of colonial life—the town hall, the church, the village common where livestock could graze in time of strife. Thus, some New England cities, such as Boston with its attractive Common, still retain an early Anglo-American atmosphere and others, such as Philadelphia and Savannah, Georgia, still show the results of intelligent colonial town planning.

Others such as New York and San Francisco grew up like Topsy allowing elbow room for the ostentatious mansions of the new rich and the slums and shanty towns of the immigrant workers upon whom many of them built their fortunes. At first most of the architecture was inspired by the old world; then social and economic changes inspired different cities to develop in different directions. Razed during the Civil War, Atlanta reappeared eventually to develop a modern sky-scraper center; prevented by post-Civil War poverty from replacing its beautiful ante-bellum and earlier architecture with fashionable Victorian gingerbread, Charleston, South Carolina, remains a charming museum to the past; New Orleans hovers somewhere in between.

Dedicated to the Grecian democratic ideals, Washington, D.C.'s designers built a new Athens by the Potomac and started an architectural trend for state capitols throughout the country; far from the influences of Europe and the east coast, and purged by the fire of 1871, Chicago rebuilt with pioneering, multi-storey, prairie-fresh architecture.

Sandwiched in on Manhattan Island, the center of New York bred a forest of steel and glass sequoia trees, reaching, always reaching, upwards toward the sun. Sprawling like a bathing beauty along the Californian beaches, Los Angeles spread outwards, ever outwards, to become what has been called 'a series of suburbs in search of a city'.

Built around enormous industrial complexes, Pittsburgh and Cleveland came firmly to agree that 'the business of America is business'; Miami Beach, Las Vegas and Honolulu's Waikiki were purpose-built for pleasure. Looking back across the Atlantic, Boston and Baltimore retained their cultural and commercial ties with Europe; built with an eye on the West, St Louis and Denver, Houston and Dallas became the new capitals of the agricultural, ranching and mining heartlands of the real middle America.

Many of these cities originally attrac-

New York's Liberty Island, (*right*) home of the Statue of Liberty, also puts the tip of Manhattan Island in perspective. The most historic area of the Dutch-settled city, it not only contains the Fraunces Tavern where General George Washington said farewell to his troops but Wall Street, Chinatown and, most recently, the tallest buildings in New York: the twin towers of the World Trade Center.

The most famous urban park in the United States is undoubtedly Manhattan's Central Park (*far right*). An 840-acre tract, it stretches from 59th to 110th street between Fifth Avenue and Central Park West. Besides its much utilized ice skating rink, its attractions include a boating lake, zoo, swimming pool, out-door restaurants and open-air theaters featuring everything from Shakespeare to 'Shake, Rattle and Roll'.

ted all economic classes: the poor huddled into crowded tenements or shanty towns, working in the sweat shops, playing in the streets and in the occasional park or playground provided by a far-sighted philanthropist or city planner, with luck hauling themselves into the middle class; the middle class living in comfortable dwellings, always improving themselves, if only materially; the rich displaying their wealth in huge mansions built along New York's Fifth Avenue, or Chicago's North Side Lake Front, or San Francisco's Nob Hill.

Then things began to change: most of the Nob Hill mansions were destroyed in the fire of 1906; urban taxes increased and servant supplies diminished; Prohibition killed many well-run old city establishments and spawned illicit night life, hypocrisy and a parasitic urban criminal element; the Depression shook America's faith in itself and its cities and destroyed the wealth of many urban-based families; the public housing schemes of the New Deal simultaneously destroyed dreadful slums and colorful old neighborhoods, replacing them with some well-designed housing and many human filing cases stacking families like research cards on top of each other; a new wave of immigrants arrived—southern, rural, under-educated, unskilled, desperate and, unlike the previous waves, black.

Land speculators, the automobile and rapidly expanding highway systems convinced the middle class that they could have the best of all possible worlds working in the bustling, executive-making city centers, living in the quiet, at least racially exclusive, if characterless, suburbs. So they became mini-pioneers: building ranch-style houses where no ranches existed; cultivating huge expanses of grass where cows were definitely not part of the scenery, wearing stetsons in the road-side supermarkets; riding herd with other motorists down the thronged, exhaust-choked motorways back into the city.

But if our cities, and their suburbs, have their defects, they also have many things to delight and charm us. We are still inspired by the architecture of Chicago and New York, thrilled by the natural grandeur of the setting of Seattle and San Francisco; charmed by the historical areas of New Orleans or San Antonio; invigorated by the vitality of almost any big American city. And in spite of their very real attractions, the suburbs are beginning to show their disadvantages: their lack of contrast and vibrancy, their stultifying conformity; their dearth of job opportunities for well-trained and/or educated housewives; their almost schizophrenic separation of men's daytime, business life and night-time/week-end family life; the often uninspired tract housing developments, the gasoline-fuel polluted motorways necessary for their existence; and, most important of all, their propensity to just grow into other cities with all the original problems and none of their compensating virtues.

There are signs that cities are noticing James Reston's warning in the New York Times: 'America is now an overdeveloped, urban nation with an underdeveloped system for dealing with its urban problems.' Community councils are finally being consulted

before drastic urban changes are made; some crime-producing public housing has been removed and more humanitarian designs may be produced in the future; environmentalists are making an impact on urban pollution; artists and dramatists, educationalists and musicians are devising entertainments suitable for the parks and streets of our biggest, more restless cities, and blacks are being encouraged—and taking the initiative—to solve some of the most challenging problems.

With luck and the new ideas of a voting age population which will be 50 per cent under the age of 40 by 1980, we may some day soon fulfill the dreams of Daniel Burnham, one of our leading urban architects. Noting that 'only a few are able . . . to live in delightful surroundings', he asked in 1910, 'but will not the people of a continuing democracy awaken sometime to the fact that they can possess as a community what they cannot as individuals and will they not then demand delightfulness as a part of life and get it?'

When Emma Lazurus wrote the famous poem for the Statue of Liberty inscription, she could not have envisaged that the huddled masses 'yearning to breathe free' might later experience difficulties with air pollution, much of it caused by the traffic which burdens our city streets, as in Broadway (*right, top*), or that 'the wretched refuse of your teeming shore' could conjure up visions of the junk yards found not only within sight of the famous statue (*above*), but across the face of our country. But if pollution and refuse are major problems for city planners, so, in New York, is the fact that one out of three of her citizens are members of a racial minority, or of a well-defined cultural, religious or ethnic group. Jews are one such group adding variety and an individual style to the city's scene, as in this street (*right, bottom*).

Some of America's most powerful industrial cities have grown up along the great waterways of the Great Lakes and their feeder rivers. The two best known are Chicago and Detroit. The hub of America's transportation industry as well as a great industrial and agricultural center, Chicago boasts (*opposite, bottom*) the lively Board of Trade which on a minute-by-minute basis determines the prices people throughout the nation will pay for groceries as well as the prosperity of millions of farm families. It also boasts some of the most breath-taking architecture in the country: three of the world's six tallest buildings, among them the awe-inspiring 1,450 feet Sears Tower; round skyscrapers such as the Marina City twin towers (*left*) built on the banks of the Chicago River; and some sixty works by Frank Lloyd Wright. Begun as a French trading post, Detroit (*opposite, top*) was incorporated into a city in 1815 but its growth and a revolution in the fledgling motor car industry were launched early in the next century when Henry Ford concentrated his attention on the Model T Ford, introducing Detroit's movable assembly lines. Now a city of 1,492,914 people, Detroit remains an automobile manufacturing center but has diversified into many other industries. Meanwhile its social and economic problems have become the most extreme example of the problems besetting many of the United States' major cities. Between the 1960 and the 1970 censuses its central city population fell by 10.6 per cent as an increasing number of well-off white citizens fled to the segregated suburbs leaving black citizens for the first time in the majority in the central city, a decreased tax base and an increased need for educational and social welfare funds. Although Detroit has been faced with unusually extreme problems, the fact that other cities face them too is testified to by the fact that fifteen of our twenty-one central cities with a population of a half million or more had lost population by the 1970 census.

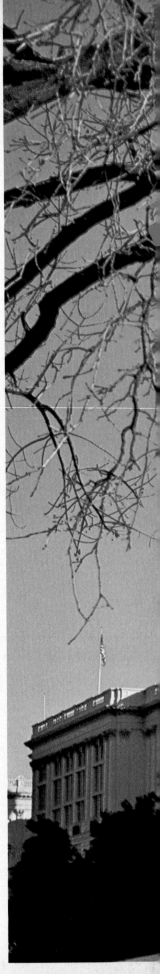

Two of America's most historic cities—Boston (*above*) and Washington (*right*)—show the different extremes of American urban architecture and lay-out. Probably the most venerable of all major U.S. cities, Boston has allowed itself to develop more or less freely, happily mixing its charming old colonial architecture and green Common with impressive skyscrapers. Thus a resident or visitor can ramble along the Freedom Trail, visiting weathered red brick buildings already well established before independence; climb up Beacon Hill to handsome nineteenth-century brownstone mansions or take an elevator to the skyscraper heights of the new Prudential or Government Centers. Washington, on the other hand, is a planned city rejoicing in the harmonious similarities of its neo-Grecian buildings. Sometimes called the Paris of the New World, it was originally laid out in the last decade of the eighteenth century by French engineer Major Pierre L'Enfant, incorporated in 1802 and then completed in its classical style after the British ravages of the War of 1812. The center of the whole carefully planned urban landscape is the

towering white Capitol building (*right*) with its great domed center and two wings housing the Senate and House of Representatives. Around it, connected to the hub by the spokes of great avenues, lie the elegant White House, home of every President except Washington, who planned the nation's capital, the Corinthian column-fronted U.S. Supreme Court building and the water-reflected monuments reflecting in their design the different personalities of three great American presidents: Washington, Jefferson and Lincoln. Sadly, among these glittering, inspiring white buildings are depressing predominantly Black slums while among the monuments of the Arlington National Cemetery across the Potomac River is the eternal flame to President Kennedy, so senselessly slaughtered. Although Washington attracts tourists fascinated by today's governing processes, Boston attracts those more interested in early American governmental processes. The capital of Massachusetts and, unofficially, of the six-state New England area, it was founded in 1630 and remains the most English of American cities, although

home to many Canadian, Irish, Italian, Polish and Russian-Americans. A major commercial port from early in its history, it was the logical seedbed for rebellion against various British trade-restricting policies. Its oldest remaining house, built in 1677, was the home of the famous horse-riding patriot Paul Revere; Faneuil Hall, called 'The Cradle of Liberty', was the meeting place for pre-Revolutionary patriots; the Declaration of Independence was read from the East Balcony of the Old State House, and from the steeple of the Old North Church lanterns were hung in 1775 to warn patriots that British Redcoats were en route to Lexington and Concord.

Philadelphia (*above*) and New Orleans (*right*) are not only thriving modern-day commercial centers but monuments to two important groups of early settlers: the English who consolidated their settlements on the East Coast, building the country's first large, independence-minded cities; and the French who spent any city-building energies they might have had in exploring and trading along the Mississippi River, finally to establish one of the country's most charming cities, New Orleans, near the mouth of the river. Philadelphia, the 'City of Brotherly Love', was founded in 1682 by the efficient, tolerant Quakers, and became midwife to the birth of a nation as well as the seat of the United States government until 1800. Among its somewhat more modern buildings is the City Hall (*above*) which covers five city blocks. New Orleans is a bustling harbor city but with a village atmosphere. Founded in 1718 and flourishing as a French, Spanish and then American city, it not only lays claim to gracious, French-style architecture but to Dixieland Jazz still found in its Bourbon street area. Recent schemes to demolish Black areas where famous jazz musicians once played to build a cultural center primarily devoted to white European-American rather than black Afro-American culture have brought protests such as the wall mural (*top right*).

When you get to Phoenix (*left, top*) this is one of the typical American sights which might catch your eye: a large saleroom of guns conveniently located next to an easy cash loan shop and a jewelry store. Another typical sight – a display of signs for strip shows (*left, below*) is found in New York City. In the minds of many Americans these two pictures are symbolic of what's wrong with our central cities: violence fed by an almost unlimited supply of weapons and the transformation of the

hearts of cities such as New York's Times Square from areas attractive to city residents to seedy crime-ridden areas of pornography shops, sex shows and prostitution. This is one reason why the big Eastern and some of the Midwestern cities have steadily lost population to the suburbs and to some of the newer, cleaner 'sun' cities such as Phoenix.

One of America's most famous purpose-built cities, Las Vegas (*above*) blossomed out of the desert following World War II. Now the largest city in Nevada, it covers thirty square miles with a permanent population of over 125,000 augmented at any given time by thousands of transient fun-seekers visiting its neon-lit Strip. So great are its attractions that it is estimated that the city plays host to 15 million visitors each year. Quite a phenomenon for a desert spot which was only

incorporated into a city in 1911. Before that it was a camping ground for the wagons and pack trains traveling over the Old Spanish Trail from Santa Fe to California, a fort protecting the Mormon mail route between Los Angeles and Salt Lake City, a ghost town, a farming community, and then a railroad division point. Its growth was expedited by the silver mines nearby and by the building of the Hoover Dam.

Writers, singers, artists, tourists have always been enchanted by the unique attractions of San Francisco, North America's gateway to the Orient (*left*). Singer Tony Bennett frequently assures us that he lost his heart in San Francisco, 'where little cable cars climb half-way to the stars,' Gene Fowler said 'Every man should be allowed to love two cities – his own and San Francisco' and President William Howard Taft simply, if not totally clearly, christened her 'The City that knows how'. Some of the things it has known how to do include developing almost overnight from a sleepy Spanish American mission station into the Gold Rush boom town of 1849; absorbing the largest Chinese population outside Asia, plus thousands of other immigrants; and producing a colorful village atmosphere attractive to socialites and Flower Children, bankers and beach boys. Confined to a 46 square mile fingertip between the Pacific Ocean and San Francisco Bay, the city numbers among its most interesting attractions various marine sights, sounds and smells: the mournful sound of the fog horns, the sight of the sweeping crimson poetry of the Golden Gate Bridge and of the busy ferry chugging back and forth across the Bay past the former prison island of Alcatraz, the smell of the fresh fish displayed along Fisherman's Wharf. The 700,000 population hub of a 4.6 million population metropolitan area, San Francisco is consequently not only the financial and insurance capital of the West but a great tourist center. Because it is built on more than forty hills the views are magnificent and the most popular form of transportation is unique: 1880s-style cable cars – America's only national monument on wheels. 'With her hills,' wrote Julian Street, 'San Francisco is Rome; with her harbor, she is Naples; with her hotels, she is New York. But with her clubs and her people she is San Francisco – which to my mind comes near being the apotheosis of praise.'

Traffic jam, Los Angeles style. The city boasts an automobile for every 2.2 persons, say the statistics – a higher ratio than for any other city in the world.

The architecture of the great cities is not the only monument one finds there to the life–past and present –of their people. The huge concrete arteries linking the suburban areas of southern California (*above*) are typical of Los Angeles, once called 'a series of suburbs in search of a city' whereas the 630-foot archway on St Louis, Missouri's waterfront (*right*) tells visitors that this is 'The Gateway to the Western United States'. The third largest city in the United States with a population of 2,782,400, Los Angeles was founded by Spanish-American explorers in 1781. It now covers nearly 500 square miles–one of the largest land areas of any city in the U.S., but its suburbs sprawl on down and up the coast helping to make California America's most populous state and the one with the highest degree (93 per cent)

of metropolitan concentration. By the year 2,000, thirteen per cent of the country's population is expected to live in the area extending from San Diego 125 miles south of Los Angeles to San Francisco 400 miles north. Supported by a great variety of industries, including air-craft and missile production, electronic and oil refining, Los Angeles is even better known for its Hollywood studios, its posh film colony residential areas, its beaches and its casual, mobile way of life. St Louis, on the other hand, has developed into a much more traditional type city. It was founded by Frenchmen in 1764 as a fur-trapping center, and because of its strategic river traffic site it became a great fitting-out center for the pioneer rush of the early 1800s. Today, St Louis remains an important interchange point for rail,

truck and air traffic as well as a manufacturing (space capsules among other things) and produce center. Besides the Eero Saarinen-designed Gateway Arch, America's tallest national monument, its attractions include the riverboats maintained along its Mississippi River front and the Old Courthouse where the Dred Scott case was tried.

Pittsburgh's Golden Triangle (*left*) is an example of what a central city can become, whereas the New York State suburb (*above*) is an example of the type of area to which an increasing number of metropolitan workers and their families are moving as central cities decay. Once known as a dirty smog-clouded industrial city, the city of Pittsburgh, center of a metropolitan area of some two and a half million people, launched a renaissance in 1950. Concentrating on the Golden Triangle of land where the Allegheny and Monongahela Rivers meet to join the Ohio, it enacted smoke and flood control measures and then razed fifty-nine acres of commercial slum property, leaving only the remains of the old fort built here by the British in 1764. In the slums' place there are now a 36-acre state park, a history museum and Gateway Center with its six modern office skyscrapers, a hotel, an apartment-office building and 750-car parking garage under a landscaped plaza of fountains, shrubs, flowers and trees. Besides other office-building programs throughout the Triangle–one-fourth of the area has been re-made–the city has developed a huge housing-production program, both in the public and private sector, both in the city limits and in the suburbs. However, many cities, through lack of funds or lack of concern, have allowed their central areas to wither under the assault of an increasing number of social problems. The 1970 census revealed that for the first time more Americans live in the suburbs than in central cities or rural areas. The trend has become so pronounced that some of the former suburban areas closest to major central cities are themselves developing some of the less attractive aspects of central city life, such as decaying neighborhoods and loss of population. However, there are signs that some big cities are making efforts to revitalize their once vibrant central areas even as there are signs that not all commuters are totally happy with their sanitary, segregated but sometimes soulless suburbs.

Poet Carl Sandburg exactly caught the spirit of Chicago, when he wrote 'Hog Butcher for the World/Tool maker, Stacker of Wheat,/Player with Railroads and the Nation's Freight Handler', for Chicago and its sprawling industrial suburbs encompassing sights like this steel company to its south along Lake Michigan, are the most powerful urban examples of America's great industrial and agricultural power. Besides its heavy industry, including iron and steel, agricultural machinery and transportation, industries based upon agricultural products remain important. Although most cattle are now slaughtered at their source, Chicago's Union Stock Yards remain the capital of our meat industry; the Board of Trade Building is a clearing-house for much of the nation's farm produce and the Chicago Mercantile Exchange is the world's leading futures-trading produce market. It is difficult to believe that Sandburg's 'tall bold slugger set vivid against the little soft cities' was a frontier outpost of less than a dozen cabins as recently as 1830. But now it is one of the cities of the future.

HISTORIC AMERICA
The Backbone of a New Way of Life

WE AMERICANS have always had a strange, contradictory relationship with our history: on one hand, more than any other nation, we've glorified the new, the modern, the instant, the disposable way of life; on the other hand, we've sanctified our early American history and what we see as its simple, non-changing values.

Thus at the same time we have preached the gospel of Man-centered materialism and revered the God-centered faith of our founding fathers; ignored, at least until recently, the duplicity of our modern public figures while insisting upon a simplistic, larger-than-life image for our early patriots; produced some of the world's largest, most futuristic cities and a vast amount of nostalgia for the small provincial towns and farms of our country's youth; allowed some of our authentic historic areas to be bulldozed away for skyscraper offices while creating putty 'historic' villages.

In the same area we can find a beautiful southern mansion converted into a gasoline station and a tasteless but perfectly maintained statue of an obscure Civil War hero; a super-highway processing people at super-speed through a scenic landscape and road-side historic markers – 1,300 in Virginia alone – begging us to stop and read yet another installment of the American Story; atomic research stations and ancient Indian pueblos; drive-in movies and a re-enactment of some great historical event; hippies, Black Power advocates and Colonial Dames.

We accept these contrasts as part of the American Way of Life. Visiting foreigners may find them fascinating, amusing or even maddening. An Englishman who regularly drinks his pint of bitter in a pub older than the United States of America chuckles at being invited to a reconstructed eighteenth-century town; an Italian who has grown up surrounded by the ritual of his church is surprised to discover during a great American parade dedicated to God and Country that God is really an American; a Frenchman who would never dream of following Napoleon's battlefield route discovers grown men dressed up in costumes recreating the Battle of Saratoga. Sometimes they remark rather condescendingly: 'after all you have so little history that you must make what you have look important'; other times, something remarkable happens: they become converted. Thus that same amused Englishman may return

Among our most cherished historic objects is the Liberty Bell, tolled to advise the world that the British colonies had decided to declare their independence. Flanked by American flags, it is traditionally kept in Independence Hall, Philadelphia; during the bicentennial celebrations its new site will be elsewhere in the Independence National Historical Park. The heart of the Park is Independence Square where mass meetings were held during Revolutionary times. The Declaration of Independence was adopted in Independence Hall's Assembly Room on July 4, 1776; in 1787 it was the site of the Federal Convention's framing of the Constitution of the United States. All round the 'City of Brotherly Love' are other historic spots: the Congress Hall, occupied by Congress from 1797–1800 when Philadelphia was the nation's capital; Old City Hall where the Supreme Court held its early sessions, laying the foundations of our judiciary system; the Library Hall, home of our first circulating library; Philosophical Hall, home of the American Philosophical Society, the country's oldest learned and scientific society; the first Bank of the United States and the Betsy Ross house where, tradition says, a Quaker seamstress made the first American flag. To be reconstructed by the bicentennial will be the home of Benjamin Franklin, that most American of our early public figures: homespun, innovative, imaginative, and undoubtedly adaptable enough to teach us a lesson or two in the twentieth century, were he alive today.

to London promoting the charms of the Williamsburg restoration; the Italian weaned on 'spaghetti westerns' may loose all restraint when faced with 'the real thing' in Dodge City or Tombstone.

Perhaps it's true that the relative lack of quantity of our history has inspired us to excel in the quality of its labeling, preservation, restoration and promotion; perhaps the freshness of our experience–and our belief in America's almost messianic calling to be a new kind of country–communicates a vibrancy lost in many older countries; perhaps the very contrast of our obsession with the future and our fascination with the past projects our history on an even larger screen.

If so, it is a projection that can prove false if we're not careful. Thus even as we of English origins visit Jamestown and Plymouth we should remember earlier arrivals in our land: the Indians who were producing great, terraced communal dwellings at places like Mesa Verde National Park during Europe's Dark Ages and four and a half centuries before Columbus discovered America; the Vikings who may or may not have left behind the Minnesota runestone carved in 1362; the Spaniards who had already established a thriving capital in Santa Fe, New Mexico, a decade before the Pilgrims arrived; French explorers such as La Salle who had traveled the whole length of the Mississippi River thirty-four years before Virginia's Governor Spotswood, first resident of Williamsburg's elegant Governor's Palace, had managed to make the 150-mile journey to the top of the Blue Ridge mountains.

As we tour through the great homes of America's industrial barons we should remember others, like Daniel Boone, the great pioneer, and James Wilson Marshall, the discoverer of California gold, who contributed to America's wealth but who were swindled of every claim. As we visit Appomattox, site of General Lee's surrender, or the romantic old plantations and cities of the South, we should recall not only the mark left on America by slavery but the mark left on the south by a brutal reconstruction. As we perpetuate the legends of those great heroes who died in the Alamo we should remember the unsung youths who died in another, more bewildering war–Vietnam. As we visit the Custer Battlefield National Monument in Montana or the National Cowboy Hall of Fame near Oklahoma City we should ponder on the Indians cruelly and needlessly slaughtered, on the frontier women rarely mentioned in the songs and legends of the Wild West. As we congratulate ourselves on our role as a 'melting pot' after visiting New York's Immigration Museum, we should recall the Freedom Riders, Little Rock, the assassination of Martin Luther King. When we stand awed in front of a statue of Presidents Washington or Lincoln we should remember that the nation that elected them also elected Grant and Harding. When we look at a copy of the Constitution of the United States or at the Liberty Bell we should speculate about the freedom to protest at Kent State University. When we photograph the few remaining buffalo or the natural wonders protected in state and national parks we should wonder about the glamorizing of the great buffalo butchers, the pollution of many of

our lakes and streams. When we browse through the atomic museum in Los Alamos, New Mexico, we should muse on the devastations of Hiroshima and Nagasaki as well as upon the peaceful potentialities of atomic energy. When we wander through Arlington National Cemetery's World War I and II graves we should stop at the John Kennedy memorial and wonder at the problems of a nation often at war with itself over such issues as Civil Rights, student protest, dishonesty in government, the controls of big business and the ability of any madman to purchase a gun and destroy the human symbol of our way of government. Finally, as we visit the Houston Manned Space Craft Center or watch another blast-off from Cape Canaveral we might be tempted to ask why a nation able to penetrate space is still unable, or unwilling, to solve many of its earlier problems right here at home.

For history is not just a list of achievements, a series of carefully staged re-enactments, a patriotically worded song or plaque; it's a path to the future. Unless we mark and are guided by our failures as well as our very great successes along the way we risk double jeopardy: an inability to find our way back to our formative origins and an inability to go forward effectively into an admirable and unrivalled third century of nationhood.

Although America's history in the minds of many Americans began when the Pilgrims landed in Massachusetts in 1620, the American Indians were already drifting onto the Continent at least 25,000 years ago, leaving behind them such cities as Mesa Verde, Colorado (right), thriving during the European Dark Ages and more than four centuries before Columbus discovered America. The Pilgrim House (above) is a reconstruction of the type of dwelling built by the East Coast's earliest European settlers.

Two groups outside the conterminous United States –the Mexicans and the Hawaiians–have left their mark on our history, folklore and art. Our history books urge us to 'Remember the Alamo', (*below*). How could we forget: the massacre of its 180

defenders in 1836 by an army of 2,500 Mexicans, besides making the martyrs an immortal part of our history, led to the independence and later statehood of Texas, and, of course, has formed the basis of numerous Hollywood films. And although the Mexicans were later completely defeated during the Mexican-American War, much of the territory and population gained retain a strong Mexican flavor. Besides surf boarding, the hula hula, pineapples and the Hawaiian guitar, our fiftieth state has contributed Polynesian art such as this totem pole (*left*) from the royal mausoleum to the artistic heritage of our country.

Although the history of our democracy began along the Atlantic coast in places like Jamestown, Virginia (*below, left*), founded in 1607 as the first permanent English colony, and although our first six presidents came from the old settled states of Virginia and Massachusetts, it was frontiersman Abraham Lincoln, who grew up in a simple log cabin similar to this one in New Salem, Illinois (*below, right*), who guided our democracy through its first great crisis: the Civil War. Today thousands of tourists visit his touchingly humble, seated statue in Washington, D.C. (*right*), and the restoration of the Illinois village in which he lived. Also popular with tourists are the ruins of the seventeenth-century Jamestown church built on the site of the meeting of the first representative body in the United States and guarded by a statue of Captain John Smith, Virginia Governor in 1608 and friend of the Indian Princess Pocahontas who saved his life and married fellow colonist John Rolfe.

The gracious style of living that was to become identified with the pre-Civil War Deep South actually began much earlier, before the Revolutionary War, in the British colony of Virginia. Restored in 1926 by John D. Rockefeller Jr, Williamsburg (*below*) retains much of the same atmosphere it had when it was capital of Virginia and the largest town in the colonies in the first three quarters of the eighteenth century. Carriages driven by men in livery carry visitors down its dirt streets, Southern belles in farthingales sweep out of its colonial homes, craftsmen continue to make wigs, candles and candy in the traditional ways; ladies with F.F.V. (First Families of Virginia) accents guide tourists through the mansion where elegant Governor Spotswood wined and dined two hundred of the colonial gentry during 'publick times'. Further north, on the outskirts of Washington, D.C., lies Mount Vernon (*right*) where George Washington was living a luxurious life with his wife, when called upon first to become Commander-in-Chief of the revolutionary army and then first President of the United States.

Old wooden Fort Osage (*above*) near Kansas City, Missouri, is typical of the forts once found throughout the Wild West and Midwest. Built in 1808 by explorer William Clark of the Lewis and Clark expedition, it was the first outpost of the United States in the Louisiana Purchase. The cleverest land deal of all times, the purchase was negotiated with Napoleon by command of President Thomas Jefferson. At one stroke of the pen he more than doubled the existing territory of the United States for a mere four cents an acre! Then Clark and a veteran Indian campaigner, Meriwether Lewis, were sent to measure and survey it, traveling past this fort for nearly 2,000 miles till they reached the Pacific.

When modern television viewers think of 'The Virginian' they think of a cowboy; when many historians think of him they think of Thomas Jefferson, erudite, innovative third President of the United States. An architect, Jefferson not only designed his own home, the lovely Monticello on a mountain overlooking Charlottesville, filling it with his own practical inventions, he also designed the capitol building of the state at Richmond and Charlottesville's University of Virginia, including the Pantheon-inspired Rotunda (*below*), housing the library and fronted by Jefferson's statue.

The gun-slingers and cowboys of our Wild West have left many legacies behind, among them a tradition of violence, an affection for guns and such picturesque spots as (top row) the site of the commemorative plaque to the famed Pony Express, found in the Rocky Mountains of Colorado; San Juan Bautista, California, with its bulletin board of nineteenth-century stage coach robbery reward posters; (bottom row) Virginia City, Nevada, where 110 saloons used to serve those attracted to its Comstock Lode of gold and silver; and Tombstone, Arizona, with its OK Corral, Crystal Palace Saloon and Boothill Cemetery, site of many a wryly-worded obituary.

Unlike some countries which have allowed their historic sites to be absorbed or even destroyed by the twentieth century, the United States still proudly preserves, cordons off and even re-enacts its history, be it of national or even international interest as is Valley Forge, Pennsylvania, (*above*), site of General Washington's encampment through the grim Revolutionary War winter of 1777–8, or of primarily local interest as is the sheriff's office in Apple Valley, California (*left*). The 'Wagons Ho!' re-enactment (*right*) is a reminder of the covered wagon caravans which crossed Kansas during the last century, leaving behind the wagon-rutted Sante Fe and Oregon trails as well as a series of famous prairie forts and such Wild West enclaves as Dodge City, the 'Cowboy Capital of the World', Abilene and Wichita, the shipping points for the cattle driven up from Texas along the Chisholm Trail.

America has always been a pioneer in the transportation business. Faced by vast distances and encouraged by an adventuresome spirit, it produced its first transcontinental railway in typical American fashion: by encouraging two companies to race from east and west toward a central meeting point. On May 10, 1869 the tracks met up at Promontory Point, Utah, provoking a hundred gun salute from New York, the ringing of the Liberty Bell in Philadelphia and the driving in of a golden spike by the Governor of California. Today, many of the railroads still exist while others, sadly, have been eclipsed by the competition of air travel or mismanagement. Here (above) the tracks down which the Chattanooga Choo Choo once chugged, lie rusting and weed covered in Chattanooga, Tennessee. Until the time of Henry Ford, America's fledgling automobile industry operated from small, slow shops, producing works like the Franklin car (below), the first American one with an air cooled engine. Then Ford revolutionized the industry by concentrating on one model, his famous Model T, and introducing a moving assembly line. Today cars like the Franklin have become collectors' pieces, Ford's Detroit has become synonymous with assembly-line, mass production methods and America is one of the world's most mobile societies.

When the great geographical frontiers of our own land were closed to us we decided to conquer the new frontier of outer space Once again, as with the transcontinental railroad, it was done as a race–this time against Russia. Space shot after space shot (right) successfully probed the universe then on July 21, 1969, came the most awe-inspiring feat of all: the spacecraft Apollo II landed men on the moon. From their balcony seats in space, the astronauts saw our world and our country in a new perspective, a perspective that we are beginning to adopt. For if we can successfully conquer space we can successfully conquer the other challenges that face us as we move to our third century of independence.

ACKNOWLEDGMENTS

The publishers are grateful to the following for the illustrations reproduced in this book:

Alabama Bureau of Publicity and Information 17 (B); Alaska Travel Division 33 (B); Aspect Picture Library 1, 82, 91, 97; Barnaby's Picture Library 59, 123 (BR); British Airways 124 (B); Vincent Brown 9 (T), 78, 79 (T), 85, 87, 102 (T), 126 (T); Camera Press Ltd 65, 76 (L), 114; Florida Department of Commerce 18 (L), 19, 127; Hawaii Visitors Bureau 34 (T); Indiana Department of Commerce 84; Kentucky Department of Public Information 69; Keystone Press Agency Ltd 106, 113; Paolo Koch 7, 39, 46, 47, 58, 60, 64 (R), 68 (L), 76–77. 80, 81 (T), 94, 103, 109 (TR), 116; Ozzie Lyons 126 (B); Minnesota Department of Economic Development 15 (T); Missouri Tourism Commission 121 (R); Ohio Department of Travel and Tourist Bureau 61; Oklahoma Tourism 67 (BR), 86 (T); Oregon State Highway Division 23 (T); Pictor Limited 34 (B), 51, 55, 83 (B), 92, 95 (T), 108; Picturepoint Ltd 4, 10, 13, 17 (T), 21 (B), 22, 23 (B), 25, 26, 27, 33 (T), 66, 74, 79 (B), 81 (B), 95 (B), 104, 117, 121 (TL), 122, 123 (TL); David Redfern 16, 71, 75 (B), 83 (T), 101 (T), 115; Rex Features Ltd 45, 105; G. R. Roberts 53 (T), 53 (B), 62 (L), 67 (BL), 98, 110–111; Spectrum Colour Library 56–57, 64 (L), 75 (T), 93, 99, 120, 123 (TR); South Dakota Department of Economic and Tourism Development 88–89; Tony Stone Associates Ltd 8, 15 (B), 21 (T), 35, 36, 37, 40–41, 86 (B); Syndication International Ltd 11, 96 (T), 123 (BL); Travel and Promotion Division, Department of Conservation and Development, Raleigh, N. Carolina 9 (B), 43 (T); TWA 124–125; United States Travel Service 24 (T), 28–29, 42, 44, 72, 73, 96 (B), 101 (B), 107, 118 (B), 119, 125 (B); Vermont Agency of Development and Community Affairs 54, 63; Virginia State Travel Service 118 (T); Washington State Dept. of Commerce & Economic Development 31, 49; Paul Watkins 32, 100; West Virginia Dept. of Commerce 43 (B); Wyoming Travel Commission 2, 20, 38, 48; Zuckerman and Baugh 102 (B).